SPECIAL ED
TEACHER MAN

SPECIAL ED
TEACHER MAN
Bob Anterhaus

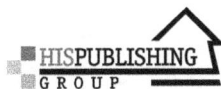

HISPUBLISHING GROUP

www.hispubg.com

A division of HISpecialists, llc

Inquiries should be addressed to Bob Anterhaus
c/o HIS Publishing Group, PO Box 12516, Dallas, Texas 75225

Published by HIS Publishing Group, a Division of Human
Improvement Specialists, llc

Contact: info@hispubg.com
Cover Design by Haeden Design Studio
Interior Design by Anton Khodakovsky

Library of Congress Control Number:
2014900038

ISBN 13: 978-0-578-13267-9

Printed and bound in the United States of America

1 2 3 4 5 6 7 8 9 10

Dedication

To Sister Cornelia, the Catholic nun who saved me from myself when I dropped out of high school.

To Joanne Ducotey Anterhaus, my wife, who liberated me when I was just a "successful failure." She was also the angel who enlisted me to become a teacher.

I dearly love you both!

TABLE OF CONTENTS

Dedication   v

About the Author   ix

Introduction   xi

1. Sam's Stupendous Sham   1

2. Reflections of My Childhood   17

3. My Vietnam Experience   45

4. Life after Vietnam   65

5. Coming on Board the DISD   71

6. Ten Week Alternative Education Program   81

7. Insights from My Training   101

8. My First Command at Walnut Hill   121

9. Moving on to Tom Gooch   127

10. Moving on to Ben Milam   143

11. Transition into Resource and Inclusion at Ben Milam   153

12. What I Learned About Autism   163

13. Moving to Retirement   181

14. Current State of Administration   191

15. General Comments about Our School System   197

16. Humorous, Ridiculous, Racy, Audacious, and Preposterous Stories   221

17. Crossing the River   241

18. From Composing Poems to Writing a Book   251

19. Last Thoughts for Now   273

Glossary   295

ABOUT THE AUTHOR

Bob Anterhaus was born and raised on the wrong side of the tracks in St. Louis, Missouri. He graduated from Southern Methodist University and holds a Master's Degree from the University of Dallas. Bob is married to Joanne Ducotey Anterhaus and has two sons, a disabled stepson, and a stepdaughter. Bob also had a Down syndrome brother who died at 27 years old.

Bob was a special education teacher in the Dallas Independent School District for twenty years. He retired in January of 2012 because his students were moved to other schools and his contract wasn't going to be renewed at the end of the school year. If those circumstances had not occurred, he would still be teaching. He taught autistic students in three different elementary schools for 11 years and special education for regular students who needed help in reading and math for nine years.

Although he didn't realize it, his many successes and failures, including dropping out of high school, all led him to become a special education teacher. He never thought he would be so successful in life and didn't think he would even live this long.

INTRODUCTION

I NEVER PLANNED TO BE A TEACHER as a young person, in fact teaching was one of the last occupations I would have chosen. Interestingly, in the process of writing *Special Ed Teacher Man,* it occurred to me that everything I experienced during my life led me toward becoming a special education teacher. All my successes and failures have been excellent tools that molded me into the type of teacher who has been able to help many students and their families. Throughout this book, I share those molding experiences resulting from my childhood, early adult years, life at Mobil Oil, and my military service in Texas, California, and Vietnam.

Below is an Email I wrote to the Editor of the Dallas Morning News on January 5, 2012 before writing *Special Ed Teacher Man.*

Dear Editor of the Dallas Morning News

My name is Robert Anterhaus and I am writing in hopes that you can recommend a capable and reputable person to help me write a series of articles or a book about my 20 years as a special education teacher in the DISD.

I taught at three schools, two of which were blue ribbon schools (Walnut Hill and Ben Milam). I also taught at Tom

Gooch. I began teaching at age 48 after my career at Mobil Oil came to an end due to downsizing in 1992. I went through the Alternative Certification Program and taught autistic students for 11 years and Inclusion and Resource students for nine years. I am retiring January 31, 2012, because my class was eliminated, and I accepted the excess employee package.

Below I have included my three minute presentation given to the DISD School Board on November 11, 2011. The presentation can also be found on the Alliance Teachers' Union web site. I gave the presentation to expose the fact that the DISD board members broke the Spirit of Federal Education Laws when they closed Milam and several other inclusion classes forcing home school students to attend other schools.

I have kept a full daily journal for the last 39 years, so I have much information to draw on. I have seen inspiring, ridiculous, humorous, tragic, common, and unbelievable things happen over the course of my teaching career. I believe what I have seen and done in the Dallas School District should be told. My desire is to tell the story, obviously for myself, but also for all my former students and for all the teachers and assistants I have known and worked with.

I've had a blessed career as a Special Education teacher. My assistants and I have helped a lot of students and parents. I would like to continue that legacy by telling my personal story of advancing from a well-paid dismal business manager to a happy, successful, professional educator.

I wrote a technical book for Mobil Oil years ago, but now would like to work with another person in order to save time. I am also not aware of publishing or legal considerations. I would be happy to meet with you, anyone on your staff, or whoever you can refer me to so I can fully explain my feelings and future plans.

PRESENTATION TO THE DALLAS SCHOOL BOARD
NOVEMBER 11, 2011

My name is Robert Anterhaus. I have been a DISD special education teacher for 20 years and have taught in 3 different elementary schools (Walnut Hill, Tom Gooch, and Ben Milam). I taught autistic students for 11 years and resource/inclusion for the last nine years. I have a degree from SMU and a Master's Degree from the University of Dallas. I was Teacher of the Year for Tom Gooch one of the years I was there.

I've been teaching the last 11 years at Ben Milam, which is a U.S. Department of Education Blue Ribbon School. Unfortunately, at the end of June last year, my class was eliminated, and in August my special education students were forced to leave Milam and go to other schools. When I first found out I didn't think this was legal. The thought occurred to me it couldn't be legal to move special education inclusion students, especially Milam's home schooled students, to other schools. They also moved the autism class, so now Milam has only one special education teacher. She is a speech therapist and comes only one day a week.

Later, I found out they could legally eliminate my class, but I still wondered if the action taken was morally right. I am concerned that no future students will be put in special education at Milam; instead they will be forced to go to other schools. There are two questions we should all be concerned about:

1. Was it just Milam or were other schools involved in the inclusion class closures?
2. Because of the spirit of special education laws, could these class closings be overruled in a Federal Court of law?

The parents and students were devastated. One student had been at Milam five years and only had one more year before completing 5th grade. Tears were shed by all, including teachers. Another student entered special education at Milam just a few months before the end of the school year and had to start a new school in August. The mother was very upset.

Tonight, we are here to think about imploding the career of over 200 teachers who have valid contracts in order to save money. Please keep in mind these are decent professional people who have families, money should not be the only reason that governs what happens.

THIS EVENING I ONLY ASK THAT WHATEVER YOU DECIDE TO DO SHOULD BE WHAT YOU TRULY BELIEVE TO BE THE HONEST, FAIR, AND MORALLY RIGHT ACTION TO TAKE FOR ALL CONCERNED.

Thank you for your attention.

\~\~\~

It wasn't included in my prepared presentation, but I spontaneously ended with, "God bless everyone here. We're all on the same side, folks." Same side meant the 100 to 200 people in the auditorium audience, which included teachers who were about to get the ax and the school board members. Giving my presentation was what I thought was the right thing to do for my students and families. Especially, since parents of the various ethnic groups, like the Hispanics, were not standing up to the school system to protect their children's rights. I felt we should all be united together in determining what would happen to our children of the future.

Sadly, I was the only speaker, which reminded me of Germany in the mid 1930's. No one dared speak up or stand up to the Nazis. Please forgive me; I am not comparing the school board to the Nazis. However, on the night of my presentation, the look in the board members eyes and their body language appeared to me as that of a professional poker player. They exhibited absolutely no feeling or emotion. My perception was that they didn't care what I had to say and were intent on carrying out their selfish agenda. Thus, I am going to share my experience in Vietnam and challenge you, the reader, to be open to the parallel between the abuses which occurred in Vietnam with the abuses I witnessed during my tenure at DISD.

I am pleased that the Morning News Editor did not answer my Email request for assistance, because I needed to tackle this project on my own. Writing the book has been a difficult labor of love. Oh, I got a few laughs and experienced fond memories reflecting back on my career, but also encountered memories that were difficult for me. Despite everything, I sincerely thank the Morning News for ignoring me, because it forced me to use my own style of phraseology and mode of expression.

Before writing the book, I knew how to express myself in writing, but as I expressed in my Email to the Morning News Editor, I knew nothing about publishing or the legal considerations. In fact, when I told my wife I was going to write a book, her first words were, "Oh no! We want to keep our lives private, and you are going to get us sued!"

Well, I am too old to care about my private life, but out of respect for my wife I have no desired to get sued. Therefore, I do not use the real names of many of the DISD personnel, especially some administrators and out of respect for my students' privacy, I have changed their names to pseudonyms. However, the names of my friends are correct, including military friends, assistants, principals and some administrators. My friends should be proud of their accomplishments, in fact we should all commend them for the work they have done. I share many of those accomplishments within this book.

Some of my Dallas School District colleagues reading this book may ask, "Why are you telling us what we already know?" To these colleagues my answer would be threefold.

1. There are many improvements that need to be made. Obviously, not everyone in the DISD will agree with what I have to say, which is sad.

2. The book will be of exceptional value to those in special education. Maybe it's a pipe dream, but I would love to touch educators from various countries. Educators and their students throughout the world share many common bonds, so it is my hope, that this book will help them and be of interest to everyone associated with education.

3. Most everyone has a disabled person in their family, extended family or a friend's family so it is my hope that the book will be of interest to the average person as well.

For this project I felt it only necessary to share my personal experiences and perspectives. Please note, if I ever decide to write another book on the subject, I plan to interview teachers, assistants, parents, principals, government officials, and last but not least, some of the DISD administrators. I will definitely interview the students, because the most in depth and momentous material will come from them. It is, and always has been, about the students! I thank God for calling me to the teaching profession and for all the students I have encountered over the years.

Now let's get started by addressing the issue of the drunken sailor who's been staggering around in the Dallas Independent School District for a long time.

CHAPTER 1
SAM'S STUPENDOUS SHAM

WHAT WOULD YOU SAY if I told you there was a drunken sailor working in the Dallas Independent School District? You might ask, "Who is this drunken sailor and how did he get into the School District? After all, isn't the DISD one of the largest school districts in Texas or even the United States?" To which I would respond, "Yes it is one of the largest districts, but to answer the question about who he is and what he is doing in the district, I would like to make a comparison by relating an experience I had in Vietnam. The story takes place in 1966 in the city of Nha Trang.

I was in a crowded bar one evening when several US sailors wearing enlisted men's uniforms came in. I did not know what rank they were, because I did not understand the U. S. Navy. After all, I'd never seen any other navy men during my tour in Vietnam. I assumed they were on some special assignment because Nha Trang is located on the South China Sea and the large US Navy port of Cam Ranh Bay was about thirty miles away.

They were already half shot (drunk) when they came in, and as they continued drinking they started to get more rowdy. It was a very small bar crowded full of US service men, a few contract civilians, and a Vietnamese staff including several bar girls wearing miniskirts. The navy guys started to banter back and forth with some army men. One sailor got up to use the hole, an actual hole in the floor referred to as the restroom, when he tripped over a chair and fell on a table where some army men were seated drinking "33" Beer. His clumsiness created a problem. "33" was a brand of beer and though terrible tasting, was the only brand the bar offered and it wasn't cheap. It cost about 100 piasters a beer, which was about 96 cents-big money for an enlisted man.

About the same time, another navy man grabbed a boy waiter and yelled that he didn't get the right change. Soon he had the lad in a headlock. The bar was run by an old looking woman who was referred to as Mamasan, the Tiger Lady, who ran over to intercede. She first told the army men at the table she would replace their beers free of charge. Her offer surprised those listening because seldom was anything free in a Vietnamese bar. Next she pried her way between the boy and the sailor and shouted something in Vietnamese. The boy responded by quickly taking off his pants and handing them to her. Then the lad just stood there in his shirt and underwear awaiting her next instruction. Through the entire ruckus most of the patrons were oblivious to what was happening. After all, they were nursing their drinks and had other priorities in mind, like the little ladies wearing miniskirts.

I was still halfway sober and sitting at a table next to them, so I was paying attention. I weighed the situation carefully not wanting to be in the wrong place at the wrong time. The Tiger Lady turned the boy's pants pockets inside out revealing they were empty. Then, she started beating the pants on the floor and shouting something in Vietnamese, which got all of the sailors' attention and soon they were bursting with laughter. Next she told them she was going to have cyclo drivers take them to get a boom-boom and then bring them back in a better mood. Cyclos were bicycle taxis.

One navy man, who must have been new in Vietnam, asked, "What's a boom-boom?"

His buddy standing next to him roared, "A damn good piece of ass; let's go!" The Navy men quickly quaffed down their beers and followed her outside to go on the adventure tour. The cyclos held two men, each sitting side by side with a driver who pedaled sitting behind them. She told the drivers what cathouse to take them to and that was the last I ever saw of them.

All in all, I think everyone was happy. The sailors got a little fresh air and something to help them calm down. The bar patrons got more "33" beer and continued to see what they could work out later with the bar girls. The shrewd Mamasan kept the money rolling in, both at the bar and at the house of pleasure, where she probably got a cut of the money spent by the men she sent there.

As for me, I soon left to get a cucumber and sardine sandwich on a small baguette from a street side vendor and took a military bus back to the base. The sandwich only cost 30 piasters or about 28 cents in US money. I tried to spend money wisely since I was living on about $85 a month. We got paid in U.S. Military currency and of the $400 I earned each month the government sent $315 to Anna Marie, my first wife, whom I will discuss later in the book. She was living with her parents in Jennings, Missouri, which was not near a military base, so our son, Rob, was born in a Catholic hospital in St. Louis, Missouri. Rob's birth cost us $25, but he was worth every penny. Unfortunately, I was not present to witness Rob's birth, because I had been shipped off to Nam two months before.

Now to answer the question, "Who is this drunken sailor and how did he get into the Dallas Independent School District?" There is a drunken sailor in every public school district; he is our own Uncle Sam. Yes, the US government! Like the drunken sailors in Nha Trang, he freely spreads his money around and insists that his needs be quickly catered to. I do not have to state what my sailor friends in Vietnam wanted. As for our good ole Uncle Sam, he wants needless paperwork, which requires high salary administrators who do not teach a single student. He wants to intrude on the teachers' time by requiring ridiculous reports, and, of course, he wants to make some unrealistic laws.

I was in Vietnam one year as a US airman, which I will elaborate on more in chapter three. Upon my return to the states I worked for several companies before joining Mobil Oil where I spent 19 years and another 20 years employed as a special education teacher with DISD. Looking back, I see many similarities between my military service in Vietnam and my teaching in the DISD System. On the positive side, I worked with many good and decent people and in both jobs did a lot of good overall. On the negative side, I saw corruption, a tremendous waste of money, bad leadership, and political blunders. Through this writing I will show these comparisons between Vietnam and DISD. I will also share places and events during my life that contributed to my successful teaching career.

At times, I will use the sarcastic expression "Welcome to the DISD," meaning in my opinion, the Dallas Independent School District has its own peculiar (and at times unethical) way of doing things. I believe that the DISD is much like Vietnam, just another third world country. Granted, it's a sophisticated one, but still it's still an inexpedient organization that I find hard to explain fully. But despite the many structural hindrances, it's my opinion that the teachers and school staffs have always done an admirable job in working with the students.

Unlike the situation at the bar in Vietnam, everyone is not happy. Only Uncle Sam and many of the administrators are happy. Many teachers are unhappy because they feel their job is to teach children, not satisfy the political agenda of Uncle Sam. I believe that some of the principals are happy because their job is partially to be yes people to the administrative system. I believe some principals do not care for parts of the present system. Unfortunately, any principal who shows concern about the setup is considered by the upper echelon not to be a team player and may have to pay a consequence. Being a principal is one of the hardest jobs I can imagine, so my intention is not to say anything negative about principals, but I believe the statement I just made is correct. To be on the team, they have to be considered a team player. I think too highly of my past principals to say they were all yes people. More probably, I could say they had to be diplomatically correct in regard to the school system and its alien policies.

I am not familiar with any school district except Dallas, but I am guessing that many other districts, especially the large ones, are similar to Dallas. They probably have similar problems in that they have too many administrators, waste funds, and spin their wheels on political maneuvers. I am also guessing that there are some very good and efficient school districts. I wish there was some way to study these districts and apply the good parts to the DISD. This idea is not original because teachers have copied ideas, lessons, and classroom structures from other teachers since day one. So why not continue the practice of studying other school systems and implementing the positive programs?

I realize this is easier said than done, and some might say we've already tried implementing programs and it didn't work. Or they might say what works in a small district won't work in such a large district. Granted some programs will not work, but it doesn't alter my point-the DISD is dysfunctional in so many ways. Let's begin the process to make it better. Maybe it will never be running at 100%, but if it's at 50% now, let's try for 60%, and when we reach that, let's go for 70%, and continue the process to keep going upward. My percentage guess of 50% may even be too high, but it's the general idea I want to convey. This sounds like a somewhat simplistic approach, but I think something that is workable is preferable to an overly complicated, non-workable solution.

Let's take this concept even further and look at the successful education systems in other countries. Many countries are ahead of the US, especially in math and science. A complete study needs to be made as to what these countries are doing right and then to determine if we can take steps to copy some of their processes and systems that would benefit our students. I know that some naysayers will say that the students in some countries attend classes more hours a day or more days a year. They may state that our special education laws and system or our multicultural challenges are holding us back. I don't know all the answers, but what I am suggesting is that we take a look at both the positive and negative factors in both our educational system and the systems of some other selected countries. We should examine positive and negative factors in an honest manner and to the fullest extent possible.

I'm sorry, if by stating the facts or offering my opinion, I have offended you, but it's high time that educational funds, both state and federal, be fully used to educate students. When funds come from Uncle Sam or from public bond issues, the money issued, oftentimes results in a blissful opportunity for DISD cash-keepers of the treasury to plunder. I won't go into it now, but it's a fact that we did have one of our DISD lady superintendents sent to the penitentiary several years ago for misuse of funds. In 2005 the DISD Technology Chief was caught in a money laundering scheme involving computer contracts. I think he was also sent to the pen, but I'm not into technology, so I didn't follow his scheme. Besides after the superintendent was sent up the river, I considered the other tricky soul's impropriety secondhand news, because it was no big surprise to me.

There were other clear-cut cases of fraud. A few years ago, many DISD personnel including administrators were using school credit cards for their own use, including buying gift cards. As I recall, one secretary was charged and the rest got off without any charges. I assume it was the Superintendent who let them get away because he wanted us to forget the fraud so the district could move forward. Welcome to the DISD.

I've seen so much money wasted. One example occurred when bond money was used to put a new roof on the Walnut Hill Elementary School. I was an autism teacher at the school. The old roof did not leak, but after they put on the new roof, water came pouring in during the first rain storm and ruined the art fair projects in the library.

Another example occurred when I was a teacher at Tom Gooch Elementary School. Five DISD employees were putting in a sidewalk right outside our room, thus, we could see them well. One man was doing most of the work while the other four were loitering. I thought, maybe the fella doing the work was new or had more energy than the others. However, later that day around 4:00 as I was walking past the auditorium I heard very pleasant piano music. I looked in the auditorium and saw the same hard working gentleman playing the piano and the four men were sitting enjoying the concert. I have no idea if they were on overtime pay, but I did know they had no business being in the school auditorium staging a piano performance. Granted this happened about fifteen years ago when times were a little mellower. In DISD at the time this activity was just a normal event that many didn't really consider abnormal. At the time, even I thought it was a little humorous.

The system we have today is putting kids at risk because Administrators are making poor decisions. To make this point clear, one day I was in a grocery store with my second wife, Joanne, who was a retired special education teacher. We ran into a lady whom she knew from when she taught at City Park Elementary School. The lady was a reading coach at the time. She related to Joanne that she too had retired from teaching, but was now a Reading Consultant for DISD making two hundred and twenty dollars an hour. Joanne's friend was a nice lady, and we were glad she could collect her monthly retirement plus earn big bucks as a consultant. We did however question the wisdom of the DISD administration in this costly arrangement. The problem was that this one case was just the tip of the iceberg, there are probably hundreds or thousands of similarly sugar coated arrangements. Maybe the DISD justifies the arrangements because the money came from some government grant. Shouldn't the bigger picture have been looked at and the monies used in a more efficient manner? It's my belief that these same arrangements continue to this day, and it is time some controls and policies are put in place to make sure our educational funds are being put to better use.

I've seen many school shams over the years, one of which occurred when I was at Tom Gooch School. The autism administrators hired two consultants to come down from Tulsa, Oklahoma, once every six weeks. One was a psychologist and the other an occupational therapist. They came to meet and examine one student at my school and one student at another school. They flew down in the morning, rented a car, spent the day at the schools, and flew back to Tulsa that afternoon. I would assume they spent additional time in Tulsa writing their reports and documenting their findings. Hiring two consultants from another state had to cost the district a lot of money. I often wondered why they hired two consultants from another city rather than use consultants in Dallas or, even better, DISD employees. Could it be because it would be more beneficial to have outsiders evaluating the case if DISD ever faced a lawsuit involving the two students? There were many DISD administrators, outside agencies, parents, and teachers involved with both students. I still don't know the reason behind hiring outside consultants, but it doesn't take a mental giant to know that the cost was tremendous.

Yes, I have seen a lot of money thrown away. Common logic for much of the waste was that the money came from federal grants. The belief was, if we don't use it, then someone else will. Let's stop a minute, folks. Let me ask a question. Who pays income taxes to Uncle Sam? All of us do, so it's a catch 22 situation. They are probably correct in assuming that if we don't get the grant money, then someone else will. Unfortunately, the common belief has become that we had better be the first one to tap Uncle Sam's colossal flow of unlimited riches.

When I first started teaching, several times I was told by the autism administrators to quickly submit a list of supplies that were needed for my class because they were applying for a federal grant. Most of the autism teachers would make a list with costs totaling $1,000 each. Whenever the administrators applied for a grant, the process would take each teacher hours to complete. The specific items we selected along with costs, vendor item numbers, and so forth had to be listed on the correct forms. Frequently, we did not win the grants so a lot of time was wasted. I guess Uncle

Sam, knowing we didn't need the money, would say, "You can fool me some of the time, but not all the time." He might add, "I may be a fool at times, but I'm not a damn fool all the time!"

Before I caught on to what grants were all about, I filed for a grant for $527.00. I was talking to another teacher about my ideas about how to help my autism students at Tom Gooch learn from outside activities away from our classroom. My field trips were always expensive because I had just a few students. Due to budget cuts at the time there was no money allotted for our field trips and the bus fare was too much for each student's parent to pay. My teacher friend suggested I file for a grant to pay the expenses and being somewhat naïve I agreed. The only good that came out of filing the grant was as a learning experience for me.

༺༚༻

GRANT PROPOSAL

A. School: Tom C Gooch
4030 Calculus
Dallas, Texas 75244

B. Class: Total Communication class composed of six students, one teacher and two assistants.

C. Amount: $527.00

D. Purpose: Community based instructions to enhance autistic students' real life community learning experiences in the three main areas of communication, social skills, and independent functioning. These will be customized to each student's individual education objectives.

E. Details:

The Science Place at Fair Park—$110.00 for bus transportation, $49.00 for entry fees

Benefits:

 a. Practice fine motor skills with use of tactile manipulation (self-help)

 b. Parallel play with peers in group activities (social skills)

 c. Increase receptive vocabulary (communication skills)

The Environmental Center in Seagoville—$110 for bus transportation

Benefits:

 a. Participate appropriately in activities involving waiting turn, sharing, and following directions (self-help and social skills)

 b. Practice good behavior in a setting with general education students (social skills)

 c. Expand abilities to appreciate nature (independent functioning)

 d. Increase task persistence and attention span in a practical learning environment (self-help)

 e. Increase receptive vocabulary (communication skills)

Samuel Farm in Mesquite $110.00 for bus transportation, $23.00 for entry fees

Benefits:
    a. Students will follow adults 2 and 3 step directions (communication skills)
    b. Interact with peers with adult supervision (social skills)
    c. Increase gross motor skills in an unfamiliar setting (self-help)
    d. Increase receptive vocabulary (communication skills)

Sunshine Day at Fair Park $110.00 for bus transportation, $15.00 for drinks and snacks

Benefits:
    a. A relaxing opportunity to mingle with neighborhood districts and community residents in a relaxed fun filled environment.
    b. A day the students can be 'free to be me'

F. Behavior: All four above community based instructional opportunities will increase appropriate behavior. This is as directed by the Tom C. Gooch Campus Improvement Plan and the Total Communication Behavior Modification Plan. When autistic students learn to control and practice good behavior opportunities learning abilities and practical independent skills are greatly multiplied.

I knew this was a good proposal and would greatly help my autistic students. The total amount of $527 was a small amount and would definitely provide the students a wonderful experience. The decision for this grant was to be made through the Special Funds Acquisition and Monitoring department of the DISD so I contacted them on the telephone, had the request typed and approved by my principal, and sent it to the appropriate person. The department didn't say yes, but they didn't say no. They just never even bothered to answer me. Interesting that much larger grants were being funded without the money directly impacting student lives. Despite what happened, I'm glad I applied because I had the satisfaction of knowing I did all that I could to help my students. Such is the strange world of grants. Welcome to the DISD.

Some of my readers might now be thinking that Uncle Sam throws money away in all directions, not just on education. I would agree that this statement is probably valid. I can quickly think of two examples. The first was the publicized bridge to nowhere in Alaska that cost millions of dollars. The second occurs every year when I file my Federal Income Taxes. I do not itemize, but with the constant changes each year I gladly pay hundreds of dollars to have my federal taxes done rather than attempt to do them myself. One year I did the taxes for my stepson Warren. I filed a simple return on the EZ form. It seemed simple at the time, but I must have done something wrong because the IRS sent Warren back a correction and a refund larger than I filed for.

I'm glad Texas has no state income tax. Each year, I tell the person doing my federal tax return that the tax system is too complicated. I relate a lot of money and time could be saved with a much simpler system minus a lot of the deductions and complicated considerations. She never really answers me, maybe because her job depends on the present tangled income tax system. The fact is that I do not know a lot about the tax system or the other money draining protrusions our good uncle rules on. I do, however, know a heck of a lot about the waste, inefficiency, and political corruption in our current education system.

Educational corruption is just one reason I am writing this book. However, it is my intention to also give credit for all the considerable good things our Uncle Sam accomplishes. I have always and still think we live in the best country in the world. That being said, let's proceed to the main reason for writing this book; the improvement of our education system.

We need to devote our full attention and funds to educate our students, but making constructive change is going to be a difficult challenge. I don't know the best way to begin, but I'm sure the usual procedure of hiring expensive consultants is definitely not the answer. I do not really know how effective it would be to start at the grass roots level with parents, teachers, and school staff because the process is so complicated. It's a beginning, but there are issues they could never resolve.

I propose starting at the congressional level by selecting a group of influential congressmen to form a high priority investigative committee. Working closely with them would be representatives from the Department of Education, volunteers from various school districts, and unpaid representatives from private industry. The industry people would be very important because they would have the necessary business and management skills, but nothing personally to gain. Specific goals and time lines would initially be established so that the project would not get bogged down or pushed aside. The committee process would need to be set at a higher priority than the way it is now with everyone complaining and making their own useless laws and accusations, much like people shooting shotguns at the moon.

In the following chapters, I am going to share my journey through life, which has been a wonderful ride that led me to the Special Education profession and my passion to express improvements necessary if we are to preserve the foundation and future growth of our present school system.

CHAPTER 2
REFLECTIONS OF MY CHILDHOOD

I HAVE TOLD MANY PEOPLE over the years that Ben Milam, one of the DISD schools where I taught, was the best school I had ever been in and that I wish I could have gone to a school like Ben Milam when I was a boy living in St. Louis, Missouri.

Saint Edwards, where I attended, was built in 1916. I was taught by nuns who were part of the Order of Saint Joseph. The Nuns were very dedicated and gave us a good education, we prayed when we got to school, before leaving for lunch, after we returned from lunch, and before we went home at the end of the day. We were also required to attend a religion class each day. The nuns lived at a convent next to the school and I don't ever remember one taking a sick day. In fact, I remember being amazed, because we never saw them go to the bathroom. Of course, they must have taken care of that business at noon when they went to the convent for lunch.

The Nuns made us work hard and were not hesitant about giving a wayward boy an attitude adjustment with a ruler. Sometimes, they would just use their hand and give us a good whack. When we received our licks, we never went home and told our mothers, or we'd get another licking. Most of the mothers stayed home during the day doing household chores and caring for their children. Amazingly, I did not know a single kid whose parents were divorced. None of my friends' mothers had a job outside of their home.

I only remember one lady who had a job and it was my Aunt Mayme. She painted ceramic statues and wall decorations and sold them out of her home. For several months she also worked days as a bartender in a tavern very near the apartment she shared with her husband Ed and their three children.

Aunt Mayme's youngest son, George, with whom I went to school for thirteen years, died at age sixty due to heart congestion. George made it through Vietnam as a member of a US Marine tank crew. His wife died at a young age so life was tough. In his last years, he developed serious medical conditions so my cousin moved in with his daughter, her husband, and their children. He was taking his daughter and grandkids for breakfast at a McDonalds when he dropped dead. It was a traumatic event for his daughter and the children, but I am sure they will always remember George as a good man and the best father and granddad they could ever hope to have.

Aunt Mayme was proud of her kids and did a great job raising them. A few years ago, before Aunt Mayme died my sister Nancy and I visited her at the senior citizen home in Florissant, Missouri, where she lived. At ninety three years old she was still alert. We had a nice visit and took some photos. Nancy gave copies of the pictures to Aunt Mayme and her two children who were still alive.

Nancy and I will always cherish that visit and the great memories we shared.

Most of the kids in my neighborhood were of German, Irish, Italian, or of Polish decent and were raised Catholic. We didn't pal around with protestant kids who went to the nearby Arlington Public School or the few Jewish kids who also attended public school. We lived in a poorer neighborhood, so other than the Catholic Schools, there were no private schools.

I went to grade school through eighth grade at St. Edwards. All the students were required to take tests in the eighth grade to see what high school they would be assigned. Since we didn't have middle schools, I was assigned my freshman year to Blessed Sacrament, a closed grade school they had converted. After my freshman year I was assigned to DeAndreis Catholic High School on Clarence Avenue in North St. Louis, Missouri. This seemed curious, because Laboure Catholic High School was closer to my house. I assumed I had been sent there because the administration had to fill both schools equally. Later I would learn many of us were assigned to DeAndreis because the way the Catholic school system was set up at that time.

The smart boys were assigned to an all-male, four year high school and the smart girls were assigned to all girl schools. As for the rest of us who weren't the sharpest knives in the block, we were assigned to coed schools. We didn't think there was anything strange about this arrangement, because anything the nuns, priests, or Catholic Diocese said was fine with us. We just did as we were told.

Unlike the Catholic High School (more on that later), in grade school, we didn't have to pay tuition, but we did have to buy our books. In order to raise funds the church held frequent raffles. Each sheet had twenty five spaces which sold for one cent each. We were encouraged to go all over the neighborhood to sell as many sheets as we could. At other times, we also sold chocolate bars at fifty cents each. On some Friday afternoons, we paid twenty five cents each to see a movie in the church basement. On some other Friday afternoons, we all brought popcorn, cupcakes, packs of candy, or other edibles from home to sell to the other students in class.

We didn't mind giving all the money we collected to the teacher for the church. After all, we could eat the various treats in class that we bought. Maybe we didn't eat very healthy, but we didn't know any better. At that point in our lives we didn't care either, but we paid the price. I had my first tooth pulled when I was in the seventh grade. My dad took me to the free clinic and I think the dentist could have put a crown on the tooth, but as I said it was free, so they put me to sleep and took out the tooth.

It wasn't until I was in high school that I started getting treatments for root canals and caps for my teeth. My dentist had his office on the second floor above a pharmacy. He was a one man operation, so he answered the phone and did appointments himself. The charge for a filling was $4 and a porcelain cap was $35. I always got the plastic cap because it was $25. I had to come up with the money for this myself, so believe me when I say that $25 was a big time expense for me.

There were no free lunches, because we didn't have a cafeteria. Most students walked home for lunch. A few brought their lunch and ate in the basement where a few mothers volunteered to watch over the kids. When we returned from lunch, we played on the cement playground if it wasn't raining or snowing.

The boys played on one side of the school and the girls the other. There was one big tree, which was on the boys' side, so we had somewhat of a scenic view. The girl's side had only the bright sun as a panorama. One favorite thing for the boys to do was to play games with football, baseball, or western character picture cards. The winner of each game kept the cards. Another favorite thing was playing tag, racing from a metal fence at one end to a brick wall on the other.

There were no volunteers or adults to watch over us. It's amazing that there weren't more serious playground accidents. I'm glad we didn't have OSHA (Occupational Safety and Health Administration). Had there been OSHA at the time there probably would have been no movement, except in slow motion, on that big cement slab. I only remember two serious accidents on the playground.

A friend named Larry tagged my cousin George hard with both hands right before George got to the wall. George's head banged into the wall, and my Aunt Mayme had to take him to get stitches. The other accident happened at the back of the playground where a low metal fence overlooked the alley. Another friend, Richie, who was in second grade at the time, fell over the fence and dropped about five feet down into the alley. An eighth grader carried Richie, who was crying, into the school. Richie had to go to the hospital and was out of school for a month.

During our free time on weekdays after school and on weekends, we first made sure we did our homework. When the homework was done, we were allowed to ride our bikes, which we took full advantage of. We did not watch television because there were only three stations, and none of the shows were any good until after 7:00 p.m.

THE SEASONS

In the winter when it was very cold in Missouri, we spent time making model airplanes or cars. Many of my friends and I had stamp collections, so we worked on our collections. In the fall, we had fun playing with all the shed leaves from the many trees. At our parents' requests, we would rake the leaves into a big pile and then light them on fire. Wow, I still can remember how we thought the resulting smoke was awesome. We would save some of the leaves and pile them into a big heap next to the garage. We would climb onto the roof and jump into the pile. Right near that garage was a large pear tree. We threw anything we could get our hands on at those pears in an attempt to have a snack. Of course, they were hard as a rock, but for us they were good eating. We also played baseball in the alley. The trick was to hit the ball straight so it wouldn't hit the garages or even worse one of the houses.

We had a lot of fun during the summer months. The Arlington Public School held programs with arts and crafts, the staff provided equipment for us to play softball, and we were allowed to play on their playground. Also during the summer we would make our own soap box derby cars. The cars were not very sophisticated, but we had fun racing them down the hills of the large streets. We also liked to take long walks on the railroad tracks. Sometimes we would build a campfire, cook baloney, and make sandwiches.

Our pleasures were fairly simple, for we had no computers or electronic games. Instead we had board games, kites, cards for poker, and marbles. I didn't like marbles too much, but I played occasionally if my friends wanted me to. In some ways we benefitted from this uncomplicated lifestyle. However, not being able to learn about technology as the kids do now, later in life when I was working at Mobil Oil, I felt like a simpleton when asked to work with complicated computer systems. Fortunately, during my teaching career there always seemed to be a teacher friend who would help me when I had computer related issues.

HAZESLEPS, MIKE'S AND FRIENDS

I said I didn't know anyone who had been divorced, but I'm sure not all the married couples were happy. The reality of life at the time was that men did not make a lot of money and the women didn't work. The women choose instead to stay home and tend to their children and wasn't uncommon to have several. Usually there was only one family car and given the fact many never learned to drive, they couldn't leave home even if they wanted to. Women would walk to the grocery store every day or two to purchase food for meal preparation. The grocery store would deliver to the older couples and those living alone.

My friend Billy was in eighth grade when he began delivering groceries. On Saturdays he would load the groceries into his wagon and then deliver them. He made twenty five cents an hour along with a few tips. On Friday afternoons my mom would send me to Hazesleps, a small family grocery store. Friday was a non-meat day for Catholics, so she would have me buy three Jack Salmon fish which cost about fifty cents. I loved our Friday fancy salmon dinners. Of course, it wasn't until many years later that I learned Jack Salmon was a cheap Whiting fish sold whole with a bone down the middle. We seldom see Jack Salmon in the grocery store, but Joanne keeps an eye out and buys some when they are available and is nice enough to cook what I consider to be one of my favorite meals. I still don't know why they called it Jack Salmon, but I do know it was good eating!

Unfortunately, when I was about fourteen, A&P and Kroger opened stores in the neighborhood and Hazesleps closed. The larger grocery stores made Hazesleps look like Howdy Doody compared to Big Tex at the Texas State Fair. From St. Edwards, it was a fifteen minute or less walk to several mom and pop food stores and corner taverns.

There was the Schaunlaus delicatessen located on the corner of Lotus and Clara Avenues. The deli was run by an older man and his wife who lived in the rear of the store. They were open from 7:00 a.m. to 9:00 p.m. Monday through Saturday and from 9:00 a.m. to 1:00 p.m. on Sunday. Then there was Mike Tighes, a typical tavern located just two blocks from our house and four blocks from my school. Mike's place was open from 10:00 a.m. to 10:00 p.m. Monday through Thursday and until midnight on Fridays and Saturdays. It was closed on Sundays.

Mike's father opened the bar and worked all day and they had a bartender who worked from 4:00 p.m. until closing. Mike frequently helped tend bar in the evenings. The tavern had an odd layout and there were always a few odd customers as well. The front door led into a small room containing a pinball machine. From there you entered a long and narrow room with a bar running along the wall and in the back was a large room with tables, television, juke box and the back door. Another room off to the side was for dancing. The television was usually tuned into a boxing match or a comedy show. Not too many people danced because they were too busy talking and drinking.

On Friday and Saturday nights the whole place reminded one of London on a foggy morning. The cigarette smoke was so dense. Remember, back in the 1950's and 60's most men smoked and only some of the women smoked. The place was not totally unhealthy, because Mike kept hard boiled eggs in a bowl on the bar. They cost ten cents each. He sold pickled pig's feet for twenty five cents each and a bag of chips would set you back ten cents.

Mister Mike, as I called him, was smart in one special way, he never touched a drop of alcohol. However, he deserved credit for keeping his customers happy. They were always drinking, eating, and drinking a little more. Mike made sure there were plenty of salt shakers spread around so the men could put salt on their egg or pig tail. Of course, many would shake a little into their beer as well. No one was going to be salt deprived at Mike's place.

Okay, you are probably wondering how I knew so much about Mike's, so I'll fess-up. It was my dad's favorite bar. He called it the corner. Before my first sister was born, mom and I would walk to Mike's late on Saturday afternoon to meet my dad. Dad started early, so he was usually at Mike's early in the afternoon.

There was a boy named Jimmy who would come to Mike's with his mother, Flo, which was short for Florence. The two of us would go outside and play. The most exciting thing happened to us one day. It was after dark and we had gone to the empty lot on the side of the tavern to play. As we turned the corner, we found what we thought was a dead man; he had his back up against the tavern wall. We immediately ran inside and told the adults. Several of the men followed us out and we led them to the stiff and to our surprise, one of the men laughed and said, "That's just one arm Gene with a load on."

Gene lived across the street from the tavern with his mother and apparently had blacked out after drinking one too many. He didn't want to go home, so he found what he thought was a concealed place to take a snooze. Everyone went back inside, and Gene continued to dream. We never asked how he lost his arm, but Jimmy and I guessed he lost it during World War II.

One Sunday Jimmy's dad got sick and my dad drove him to the local hospital. Mom and I caught a ride home with friends, Lowell and Verna. I don't know what happened, but Jimmy's dad died that day. Jimmy still came to the tavern with his mom and she became the girlfriend of another customer with the last name Miller. Unfortunately, Miller was married and had a daughter about my age. I knew Miller fairly well because he, my dad, and I went rabbit hunting together. For some reason I never knew his first name. He hung wallpaper for a living and put up red wall paper in our living room.

One day dad told us that Miller had taken Flo, his wife, and daughter out to dinner the night before. He was driving the panel truck he used for work and hit the side of a bridge. When they hit the driver side door swung open and Miller's foot got caught under one of the pedals. Back then there were no seat belts and he fell out and was dragged by the truck to his death. No one else was injured.

These questions remain: Why was he taking both ladies together with his daughter out to dinner? Was Miller drinking that night? Was there some sort of altercation in the truck that caused him to lose control? All we know for sure is that Flo lost two men within a year, Miller's wife lost a wayward husband and the daughter lost a good father whom she dearly loved. After the wreck Jimmy and his mother moved so he never returned to the tavern.

I sure missed my "saloon pal." I would watch the television, read my school books, or just sit at a table and listen to my parents talk to Lowell and Verna. I didn't like to go outside by myself. I did drink my share of sodas and ate a lot of chips at Mike's, but I'm sorry to say that I never had a hardboiled egg or pigs tail. As a matter of fact, I've never had the pleasure of eating a pig's tail. So I think I will just have to add eating a pig's tail to my "bucket list."

Sundays, the bars were closed, so oftentimes men would take their families to Floods Field, a nearby recreational park. The men would sit around drinking beer and playing cork ball while the ladies visited and prepared the food. All us kids just ran around and played.

Cork ball was a fun game. Holding a broom stick you would try to hit a small, hard ball that was pitched very fast. If you swung and missed and the catcher caught the ball or if you fouled the ball you were out. Any ball hit in front of home plate was considered a hit; however, there were no home runs.

I had a pretty good arm so I enjoyed those games of cork ball. This reminds me of an incident with Donald, one of my friends in the fifth grade. We were out of school for the Christmas holidays and I had been to confession. When I emerged from the church Donald was across the street. We started joking back and forth and I don't remember all of what was said, except that he dared me to hit him with a rock. He then stood up upright, motioned with his hand and did not move. Protecting my foolish pride, I picked up a small rock and heaved it. Whoa! It hit him in the head, and blood shot out. Neither one of us had planned for that to happen.

Fortunately, except for his pride, Donald was not seriously hurt. So I took off running and he took off running each of us going in the opposite direction. I don't know what Donald told his mom. I do know in our current culture the incident might have resulted in a lawsuit or at the very least Donald's parents pressing charges and suggesting I spend some time in juvenile detention. I decided not to return to the church for confession. How do you tell a priest you innocently clobbered one of your friends acting on a bufflehead dare?

One of my saddest moments came when I was in the fourth grade. The brother of a good friend was killed right in front of the convent. The convent faced Maffit Avenue, a small narrow street and there was a small mom and pop grocery next door. My friend lived across the street with her parents and two younger broth-ers. One evening, just before dinner, her mother sent one of her brothers to the store to buy a loaf of bread. He ran between two parked cars into the street and was hit instantly killed. My mother knew the boy's mother, so we went to the funeral parlor. A lot of people, including the nuns, were there. It was such a sad time for the whole school. The entire parish mourned.

My time at St. Edwards was spent with many of the same kids, because most people did not move from the neighborhood. My best friend, John Minoge, was the sole exception. John spent one year at St. Edwards. He came over from Ireland to live with his aunt and her two children. His aunt lived just five houses down from us on Lotus Avenue. She had enrolled him into our school. The first time we met, I was outside our house on a Friday evening. John walked by and for some reason we got into it and started wrestling. I don't remember what was said or why, but we started wrestling in my yard then rolled down the sidewalk into the street gutter. After quite a long tussle we were sweating and covered with dirt.

Still clasping each other we decided to take a break at which time we started talking. We became instant friends and from that point on were frequently seen together in and outside of school. I learned a whole lot about Ireland and how to drink hot tea. I don't know what happened, but one day John was gone. Apparently, on short notice he was sent back to Ireland. I wasn't able to tell him goodbye and had no idea what city he was from. When I visited Ireland years later, I thought of John and wished there was some way to contact him. I guess many today would ask, "Hey have you ever heard of Facebook?" My answer would be, "I hope to get around to it in the next decade."

RELIGIOUS ACTIVITIES

St. Edwards, like all Catholic Schools at that time, had many religious activities. All students were expected to attend 9 a.m. Sunday mass in the church basement. Each class sat together along with their teacher. If a student was not present, he or she had to bring a note from a parent on the following Monday explaining why they had been absent. Fortunately, I was in the choir so I didn't have to attend. Our choir sang at 11 a.m. in the high mass at regular services upstairs in the church.

During Lent, which lasted six weeks, we were encouraged to go to 7 a.m. daily mass before school. We had to fast in order to receive daily communion, so we ate breakfast in our classroom. A few brought breakfasts from home, but most of us got our breakfast from the small store across the street from school. For twenty cents we would get a Coke or Pepsi and three donuts. If we wanted to vary our diet, we could get a Twinkie or some other ten cent cake. For a mere twenty cents we got our full share of sugar.

In May, each day, the students brought flowers from home and put them in vases, which were placed in front of a statue of the Virgin Mary in our classroom. On the last Sunday in May, in the afternoon, all students went to school and walked in a procession to the statue of the Virgin Mary outside behind the church. We sang songs as we marched.

I think you now have a pretty good idea how our lives revolved around our Catholic schooling. When I was in eighth grade, our teacher picked several boys to be trained as altar boys for mass. I was not picked, but my cousin George and my friend Jimmy were selected. We thought they were lucky because they got off school to serve at funeral masses where they even earned a little money. They didn't think they were so lucky when the funeral or wedding was held on a Saturday and interfered with play time.

We always had two or three priests in our parish, and they each stayed for several years. I honestly don't think any of our priests ever did anything wrong. There was one younger priest who liked to pal around with the girls. My dad would tell my mom he was up to something. My mom just said, "Priests didn't do that kind of stuff." So Father Huhn, and rightly so in my Mother's eyes, remained innocent until proven guilty. However, there was another priest who did run off with his secretary. I don't know exactly what happened, but I'm thankful she was an adult woman and not a minor girl or boy.

I feel it is unfortunate how many priests in countries all over the world have been caught over the last several years taking sexual advantage of young boys. I am of the opinion that priests should to be able to get married. It seems to work well for the Protestant ministers to have a wife and a family. I think a lot of the old beliefs have turned off a lot of Catholics over the years. But in the Pope's defense, caught between a rock and a hard place, he has to uphold hundreds of years of Catholic Church tradition and beliefs. One question people have asked over the years, "Will females ever be allowed to be priests?" I do not believe I will see it in my lifetime, but it may occur sometime in the distant future. I wouldn't be at all surprised if the church loosened some of the rules, but who knows when that will be.

THE NUNS

I still have my class pictures that were taken once a year at St. Edwards. You can tell how hard the nuns worked by the number of students in each class. My first grade class had 28 students, second grade 42, third grade 46, fourth grade 47, fifth grade 41, and seventh grade 44. Over the years in the three different DISD schools where I worked the regular education classes had between fifteen to twenty two students. With so many students, it's no wonder that the nuns never missed a day of school. There wasn't anyone to fill in for them. I don't know what the nuns did in the summer. Maybe they got some leave time to visit their families. Whatever they did, the dutiful nuns definitely deserved some rest in order to get ready for the next school year.

When I was in one of the lower grades, an older nun who taught eighth grade, died. Her body was laid out in the parlor of the convent. She was holding a rosary, common at most Catholic funerals. It was the first time any of us had been allowed in the convent. Each class walked through the parlor past her body. The adults told us that she had a "good death." If a person lived a long life and did not suffer at the end, it was said to be a "good death." I haven't heard that expression for many years." She had been able to teach up to the time of her death and was doing what she wanted to do in life, serving her God and helping a lot of people. During that era, it was not uncommon for people to die young due to the poor state of medical treatment. Others died as a result of the many hardships and hard lifestyles they endured during World War II and the Korean War.

In all my years at St. Edwards, I believe we had only one teacher who was not a nun. Her name was Ms. McGuire and she was my third grade teacher. She was in her late 40's or early 50's and always wore a plain dress. She never spoke about her personal life, but we knew she did not have children. I'm guessing she was not married. Ms. McGuire was an excellent teacher. I would rank her alongside the excellent DISD teachers we have today.

Of course, she and the nuns did not have the teaching resources we do now. For example, we never went on a field trip the whole time I was in grade school and high school. The nearest thing we had to a field trip was the school picnic at St. Edwards. The picnic was held at the Chain of Rocks Amusement Park always on a day toward the end of the school year. The students and their mothers each paid fifty cents to ride chartered busses to and from the school. Most mothers took a picnic basket for lunch. My mom always took fried chicken, which she would make early in the morning. We saved up to pay for the amusement park rides. There were foot races, and the boys enjoyed shooting each other with water pistols.

St. Edwards didn't have extracurricular activities for the boys and girls. There were no sports programs or gym periods. The boys did have the option of joining a Boy Scout troop which met in the school basement on Thursday evenings from 8:00 to 9:30 p.m. I was a member from sixth through eighth grade. There were approximately twenty boys in our troop. Only two of the boys had full scout uniforms, the rest of us wore a shirt or a shirt and hat. Two of my friends, Jimmy Spalding and Billy Lineback, were also in the troop, so it was a lot of fun to go together.

We went on two weekend camp outs a year, one in the fall and the other in the spring. We went to a large scout area and slept in tents owned by the school. The local Scout leadership conducted a weeklong camp in the summer, but only a few boys went because it was too expensive. At $15 for the week, which was a substantial amount of money at the time, I did not even bother to ask my parents to send me. I was proud to be a member of the Boy Scout troop. I have only good memories about my time in the scouts.

I recently visited the Boy Scout Museum at their national headquarters in Irving, Texas. The original Norman Rockwell paintings depicting Boy Scouts were amazing. They conduct hands on activities for both kids and adults which add to the fun. The whole museum is interesting.

All the previous eighth grade classes had a graduation ceremony in May at the church's high mass on Sunday. For some reason it was decided that our class would be the first not to have this ceremony. Instead the mothers club had a dance for us in the school basement on a Sunday evening. My friends and I weren't too keen on the idea, but we had to go because our moms were going with us. I didn't know how to dance, so my mom taught me a dance she called the two-step before we left our house. My friends and I decided the dance wouldn't be much fun, so we planned to hang around outside and in the school bathroom. When the dance started, one of the mothers grabbed her son asking him to dance and then quickly handed him off to one of the girls. After five guys had been shanghaied, we had had enough, so we each grabbed the nearest girl to dance. We danced all night with the various mothers and the girls in our class. It was fun and exciting.

None of the guys I knew had a girlfriend like many of the kids today. Maybe we were backwards, but not having a steady was financially cheaper and sure simplified our lives. If you were to ask me, "Would you go back in time, given the opportunity, and liven things up a bit by taking a girlfriend?" My first response might be, "I wouldn't have minded complicating my life with a girlfriend or two." However, I would be more likely to say, "An intriguing question--my answer is yes and no." Due to the fact that throughout my life many things that at first appeared to be bad turned out to be good.

THE NEIGHBORHOOD

Our neighborhood was safe during the time I was in St. Edwards. I didn't see or hear of any drug use and I never knew of a single home or business burglary. The only incident I remember was when our landlady, who was elderly and widowed, had her purse snatched. She was walking home alone from the movies when someone grabbed her purse and took off running.

Everyone loved to go to the movies because the theatre was air conditioned. None of the homes had air conditioning. In the summer we would sleep next to the front door which only had a screen door, or in the back yard with mosquito lanterns, or near a large open screened window in the basement where we kept our wood to start the coal furnace. Of course, the movies were inexpensive, not like they are today, adults paid sixty cents and children paid twenty cents. Soda cost a dime, candy cost a nickel, regular pop-corn cost fifteen cents and you paid a quarter for heavily buttered popcorn. From my house, in fifteen minutes, I could walk to three different theatres, the Victory, Wellston, or the Rio.

However, good things don't last forever; it wasn't long before the neighborhood began to change. Currently in the United States we have a very multicultural society, but there was not much diversity in St. Louis in the late 1950s. For instance, to my knowledge, I don't remember seeing a Hispanic person the first nineteen years of my life. We mostly had white, black, and a few oriental people. After my grade school years there was a shift from an all-white to mostly a black neighborhood.

Traditionally, most of the blacks lived in their own part of the city. However, at the time, many blacks seeking employment were migrating north to live in big cities like St. Louis. Our neighborhood was old, but it was better than many of those traditional neighborhoods and we had good transportation and shopping. Once the blacks started moving in, many of the whites left, which caused properties values to diminish. Of course this made homes cheaper to buy or rent. I didn't fault the blacks for attempting to better themselves and their families. But, I was sad that the neighborhood I had always known was changing.

The whites left and bought new homes in the suburbs and their children benefited because the suburbs offered better school systems. Sadly, but true, most of the whites who left didn't want to live among the black people. Enrollment of blacks increased in our public schools and in our Catholic schools. In the Catholic Schools I attended, we all seemed to get along fine, probably because the nuns didn't put up with anyone being discriminatory.

My dad was one of the few whites who wouldn't move. He told our family that our landlady, who lived next door, was going to leave us the house to us when she died. She did not have any children of her own. Personally, I always thought there were other reasons for us not moving. For instance, rent was only $60 per month and the house was close to dad's various construction job sites. If we had moved, at the time, dad would have been forced to make a long commute. Of course, I already shared how much he liked Mike's tavern, which was near our house. Soon we would learn that Mike, also wanting to leave the neighborhood, had sold his establishment.

After all of my friends moved, on weekends I would hitchhike out to my cousins' home in Flordell Hills, Missouri. My Uncle Ed and Aunt Helen were very kind to let me stay because they had five children and lived in a three bedroom home. My cousin Eddie was my age and Tom was two years younger so I able to make a lot of friends in their neighborhood.

There were times dad would take us to look at houses. I'd get excited about the prospect of living in a nicer area and getting to go to a better school. With my dad moving was akin to a "Pie in the sky" along with many other things he told our family. One time he said we were going to move to Australia because there was construction jobs there for him. When I was in the eighth, ninth, and tenth grades he would tell me how he was going to procure jobs for me during the summer with his tavern friends, Speedy and Ray, brothers who had their own small construction business. Another time, he was going to let me barbecue meat in the tavern parking lot and sell the food to the tavern customers. I guess it was the alcohol talking, because I don't remember him following up on any of his pronouncements. However, he made sure I knew the words to the unofficial St. Edwards theme song. "Give a cheer, give a cheer, for the nuns who drink the beer in the cellars of gold ole St. Eds. They are brave and they are bold for the liquor they can hold. That's a story that's never been told."

My father made it through the fifth grade during the depression and worked construction as a cement mason. Over the years, he was frequently out of work due to poor weather, union politics and strikes, and personal issues. He constantly suffered from high blood pressure, arthritis, and heartburn. Smoking cigarettes, drinking alcohol, maintaining a poor diet, and lack of exercise probably accelerated these health issues, ultimately causing heart attacks, cancer, and diabetes. He stopped working at fifty nine years of age.

At the end of his life he was very ill and I was living in Dallas. He had been turned down for disability so I contacted a US congressman from my dad's district in Missouri. I communicated with his congressman for several months and was able to secure dad federal disability for his past and present medical condition. Unfortunately, he died young at the age of sixty nine.

THE MOVE

My family, finally moved early in 1961, I was a junior in high school. Our Aunt Marcella was always concerned about the change taking place in our neighborhood. She feared for the safety of my two younger sisters so she gave my dad $400 for a down payment to buy an older home in Jennings, Missouri. At that time $400 was a lot of money. The house, with woods out back, looked like a castle to me. When the day came for our move, I took off from school and helped my dad and Joe from the tavern load a small U-Haul trailer. We made several trips to the new house

About a year after we moved, we found out that our landlady had died. My dad had been wrong about her leaving the house to us. Many people, like our former landlady, didn't have a will. So, based on state law, the estate was to pass to the next of kin. Apparently the state contacted a second or third cousin or some other relative and they inherited her estate.

The title of the theme song for the popular television show The Jefferson's was, "Movin On Up." Well, in my family's case, we too were moving up to Jennings, located on the border of St. Louis. I could have chosen to attend Jennings High School only ten blocks from our house, but not knowing anyone I decided to remain at DeAndreis Catholic High School. Coincidently, Anna Marie, my future wife, attended Jennings. Since she was a year older she would have been a grade ahead of me.

DeAndreis Catholic High School where I was attending required each student to pay an annual tuition, the cost of books, and other fees depending on their grade level. My sophomore and junior years the base tuition was $125 and in my senior year the base tuition increased to $150. I had decent grades in high school and liked school, but struggled to come up with the money. I hitch-hiked to and from school to save money and would go to the library and do without lunch when I didn't have the forty cents. Along with a lot of other kids I caddied at the Normandy Golf Course. I hitchhiked to and from the course on weekends saving the bus fare, which was twenty five cents each way. I had to get to the course early to secure an "18 hole loop," commonly referred to as a bag assignment, from Eddie the Caddy Master. All the kids had to compete with the adult men who caddied for a living and were also waiting for a loop. Carrying a golfer's bag for eighteen holes took about four hours and paid $3. The affluent golfers owned heavy bags, which were tough to carry up all the steep hills. Sometimes I would be given a "double" which meant I would carry two golfers' bags and make $6 a round.

Caddying was a good way to earn money. Normandy was a private course full of good golfers who were financially well off. Most members were good to the caddies and would even buy us a soda at the tenth hole refreshment stand. If we were lucky, at times we would get a free hot dog.

I still remember the first time I caddied. I arrived to the course about 8 a.m. and spoke to Eddie. He told me to sit down on the long caddies' bench and wait my turn. Finally at 1 p.m. Eddie called me over and told me to take Mr. Florida's bag. Mr. Florida was an elderly gentleman who only played nine holes. Apparently, Eddie had told him it was my first time to caddy, because Mr. Florida kept telling me what to do. Mr. Florida gave me two one dollar bills for the nine holes and I paid Eddie my fifty cents for caddy badge number 137. That day was the first of many long, but good days caddying.

There were times I would hitchhike over to either Norwood or Glen Echo Country Clubs to secure a loop. One summer week I caddied in an amateur tournament being held at Glen Echo Country Club. My golfer won the tournament and the two of us were filmed for the nightly TV news as he was making the last putt on the final hole. He paid me $45 for the seven days. That was a lot of money for a fifteen year old to make in one week, but in no way was it easy money.

Unfortunately, with all my other expenses I hadn't earned enough to pay the annual school tuition. Not knowing what to do, I was influenced by two of my friends who also lacked the necessary funds. One was always saying he wanted to join the marines when he turned sixteen. Sure enough, his parents signed their approval and he joined the marines on his sixteenth birthday. The other friend, who was older, got his girlfriend pregnant. I do not know all the events, but somehow he ended up in court in front of a judge. The judge gave him a choice of going into the army, marrying his girlfriend or going to jail. He decided to get married because apparently he believed that love was much more preferable to war and definitely fancied marriage over doing time in a house of correction.

So at the end of my sophomore year I decided it was time to quit and join the army. It was not mandatory at the time to have a high school diploma to join the military. So I decided the military was my best option. It was a different world then. I think some things were better when we lived in such a simplistic and non-technical world. The question might be asked if I would like to return to that way of life. My answer would definitely be, "No way!"

There were many people who influenced my life, but Sister Cornelia will always be one of the most cherished. In 1960, my sophomore year, I was assigned to Sister Cornelia's homeroom and history classes. Knowing my monetary dilemma, she always encouraged me to stay in school. She would be the person God used to come to my rescue.

Sister Cornelia telephoned one day at home and asked me to come see her at the convent where she lived. It was located next to the high school. As I sat in the parlor waiting for her, I had no idea what she wanted, but felt if she had time for me, I had even more time for her. When she came in, we exchanged pleasantries, and then she made me the best offer I could have hoped for. She told me she had secured a two week job for me doing inventory in the pharmacy at Christian Hospital. The hospital was older, smaller, and one block from our school. It was also the place where I had been born. She told me the job paid seventy five cents an hour and that over two weeks I could make $60 before taxes. Without hesitation I said, "Yes!"

For the next two weeks I counted all the medications on the many shelves and in the refrigerator. The job was socially awkward for me at first, especially eating lunch in the cafeteria with pharmacists, doctors, and nurses. However, the pharmacists were nice and treated me well, so I felt comfortable. At the end of the two weeks, the chief pharmacist asked if I would like continue working part time after school and on an occasional Saturday. I accepted his offer and spent the next three years working at Christian Hospital. I worked in the pharmacy, purchasing store room, accounting office on Saturdays, and once a year in the X-ray department. After two years, I received a raise to one dollar an hour, which was equal to what some of the adults were making. Low pay was normal because the hospital was a nonprofit organization. From my prospective, a dollar an hour sure beat carrying a heavy golf bag for four hours.

I do not know where my life would have led if I had not returned to finish high school, but I do know that Sister Cornelia's kindness and dedication truly shaped the rest of my life. As a young adult, I wrote to thank her. She wrote back and said she was pleased that I turned out the way I did. She told me she had gone through some changes in her life as well and had become a librarian. I didn't dare ask what compelled her to become a librarian. I would hope that after all the encouraging words she offered her students she took a look at her own life and finally gave herself permission to do what she loved.

There was a bus that stopped right in front of my house and went within three blocks of DeAndreis, but I didn't take the bus because it cost a quarter to ride and I could get there much faster hitchhiking. Later, I was able to save up enough money to buy my first car, a 1950 Plymouth. I would drive it to school, that is, when it was running.

I owned various cars before I went into the military. My second car was a 1952 gray car. The previous owner had painted the car with a regular paint brush, but the car ran well, so I paid him $50 for it. The third car was my dad's 1954 Ford and was a real lemon. The fourth car was a 1938 Chevy, which had the car battery located under the floorboard right at the driver's feet.

My last car was named "Woody." I was attending the Air Force technical school in Amarillo, Texas. I was given a three week leave so I wrote my dad and asked him to buy a cheap car that I could use while I was home. I sent him $90, which I knew would be enough cash to get a car. Dad, or as I sometime called him, ol' Hank, out-did himself. He bought me a Pontiac station wagon with wooden side panels for $65. So we named the silly looking car "Woody." The car ran well and had plenty of room for my friends. We had a lot of fun.

In the evenings I took Anna Marie out and she never had one bad thing to say about Woody. Woody was a unique vehicle. It even had a built in beer cooler. The spare tire was missing, but the void created was perfect for icing beer. The melting water drained out through a hole in the bottom of the car. I'm sorry we never took a picture of Woody, but we were just too busy frolicking. After I returned to the base dad sold the car for $65 the same price he had originally paid.

MY SENIOR YEAR

In my senior year at DeAndreis High School the senior prom presented me with a challenge. All senior guys were expected to attend the prom with a date. Neither I, nor my cousin George, knew who to ask. So we turned to a mutual friend, John, about securing us dates. John lived near school and was in several school organizations, so he knew most of the girls. When we approached John, he asked us what type of girl we wanted to go out with. We told him it didn't matter as long as they were of the feminine order. John just laughed and said, "George, I think you want a blond, and Bob you're tall, so why don't we fix you up with a tall gal." John's assessment sounded good to us we nodded our agreement and he fixed us up with a couple cute junior girls. George's date was cherubic dishwater blond and fairly good looking. My date was tall alright and had a pretty face, but John didn't tell me she was built like a football player.

I borrowed the pharmacy boss's new car, and George and I double dated. The dance was held in the school gym, and the evening went well enough. After the dance, along with a number of other people from school, George, myself and our dates drove to the Italian section of town to a well-known steak restaurant. The food wasn't especially good, but the place was trendy and we thought it would be fun to follow the herd. Afterwards, we took the girls home, and I think we got goodnight kisses. Anyway, George and I fulfilled our school obligation by attending the senior prom with our "pinch-hit" dates.

SPIRITUAL CONFUSION

As with the rest of the kids my life seemed to revolve around school, church, and the Catholic religion. As children, we had accepted all we were told and taught. Our parents appeared to as well or at least they made us think they did. We were taught to abstain and treat woman with respect. I remember only one couple my age dating hot and heavy. Unfortunately, the girl got pregnant and both of them quit school their senior year. For the most part, my time spent in Catholic schools growing up was okay. The years were good in the sense that I increased my knowledge by being exposed to a solid academic experience, but in other ways the time was detrimental because socially I became sluggish and backward.

As I grew older, I began to question many of the Catholic beliefs and ceased to follow the sacred affirmations I had solemnly believed in at St. Edwards. Divorce became one of the biggest issues of my confusion. As related earlier, growing up I didn't know anyone who divorced. Yet, after thirteen years of marriage my first wife left. Her leaving was a shock to me, but we both knew the marriage was over. Within a few months we mutually agreed to divorce. The event had a profound impact on my life and my beliefs. I thank God for introducing me to my current wife, Joanne, who I have been married to for twenty nine years. The two of us agree that we will make it to the end or as our Baptist friends say, "Until the good Lord takes us home." One divorce was one too many for me.

I would like to relate an experience that shows how my personal feelings about those unquestionable religious beliefs dwindled as I became an adult. The year was 1977 and I was attending graduate school at the University of Dallas in Irving, Texas. I took a marketing course and along with fifteen students and two teachers I got to spend two weeks traveling to Rome, Italy, and Athens, Greece. We went to the Vatican, Parthenon, museums, and tourist places and had various guest speakers.

Someone was able to arrange for us to have an audience with the Pope in the Vatican. Our group along with a few other small groups was escorted into a small chapel. Pope Paul VI walked from the back of the chapel down the aisle to the front. I was situated just a few feet from him as he walked by. He addressed us in several languages and gave us his blessing all of which took about twenty minutes. It was a precious event, but I didn't feel overwhelmed by this rare opportunity to be so close to the Pope. There I was in the presence of the Pope just a young adult harboring diminished views of the teachings I had been exposed to as a child.

Had I known when I was attending St. Edwards that one day I would be sitting just a few feet from the Pope, I would have been the happiest kid in the world. In fact, I might even have perceived the event as gaining access to the key to the heavenly gate.

However, when we got back to Dallas, along with the other students I prepared an international marketing research paper in order to get my three hour course credit. I related the experience, but only in such a way, that it was beneficial and significant to earning my Master's Degree.

CHAPTER 3
MY VIETNAM EXPERIENCE

I DIDN'T REALLY WANT TO ENLIST in the military, but there was a draft system in place, which made it hard for me to get a job. At the time, I was not enrolled in school so potential employers assumed I would be drafted. I learned this in a roundabout way when I applied for a job at a local flour mill. I had a good interview and was told that I would be ideal for the position because of the courses I had taken in high school and college. The person interviewing me gave me a tour so I could view the work environment. To my dismay I was not offered the position. A few days later, I saw my cousin who was a secretary in the mill office. She informed me that I was not hired because of the uncertainty of my draft status. No one in personnel at the mill had bothered to notify me, I guess she was given the bad news task to tell me.

I ended up enlisting with two friends, Eddie and Jerry. Eddie became an aircraft mechanic, which he had asked for and Jerry became a military policeman, which he did not ask for. I was told by the recruiter that I could be a radio operator in the communication area, so I signed up. Eddie was shipped out the day before Jerry and I were sent for basic training. I don't know how recruitment is done now, but in the 1960's, it was all about a recruiter meeting a quota. We had signed up to do a so called "buddy plan," which meant we would all go through basic together. Looking back I am sure the recruiter never intended for us to go through basic together. He baited us to ensure his induction quota was met.

I learned a lot in the military but not much in the way of formal training. When I arrived at Lackland Air Force Base in San Antonio, Texas for basic training I was given a communication test. Prior to testing I was given a quick lesson on how to interpret a coded message. The test consisted of several dots and dashes delivered audibly through a headset. Of course, I knew nothing about Morse code and failed the test. Next I was given a general aptitude test, which showed my highest score to be in the administrative field. Soon I was assigned to be an inventory manager in the base supply system. I went to ten weeks of schooling at Amarillo Air Force Base in Amarillo, Texas.

At Mather AFB in Sacramento, California, I worked in Document Control for one year and in Base Inventory for one year. I was also assigned to the Base Radiation Team and received training how to use instruments to measure for radiation. We attended a monthly meeting and sometimes practiced using the instruments. We had B52 bombers at Mather, and I assume they must have carried some potent radioactive material. Luckily none crashed, so our team, which consisted of ten airmen, never had to get out our little Geiger counter like gadgets for actual use.

After two years at Mather, I was assigned to Nha Trang AFB in Vietnam. We flew out of Travis Air Force Base in Northern California. The chartered World Airliner stopped in Hawaii first and then we went on to Guam. In Hawaii, it was dark and we were allowed to get off the plane and walk around the airport. In Guam, it was also dark, and there was a severe rainstorm. We stayed on the plane for about an hour and then it took off in the heavy storm. We got to Saigon by mid-morning and when I stepped off the plane, it was already very hot. Later it rained, and when the sun came out again it felt like I was in a steam bath.

An airman told us we would be in Saigon for a few days to process in country. When we weren't processing there would be assigned jobs for us to do. I do not know what everyone else had to do, but I was assigned to the personnel building next to our barracks. My job was debatably not too important. I was told to take four forms, insert three carbon sheets in between them, and then staple them together. I did this on and off for two days. Keep in mind, in those days, we didn't have personal computers or word processing equipment. Not too far in the distance, I could see F-4 fighter planes taking off, so at least it appeared that some people were doing something constructive to carry on the conflict. On the third day, I and some others were put on a C-130 cargo airplane and flown about two hundred miles north to Nha Trang Air Force Base. When I got off the plane, my first thought was how beautiful the forested mountains were.

I and the other airmen in our group were taken to a small building where a military policeman spoke to us about thirty minutes. He gave us some general information about the Nha Trang area. I remember him well because he was missing some of his front teeth. He told us his jeep hit a big hole, and he was thrown out. Jeeps had no seat belts in those days. After that meeting, sergeants from the various units picked us up, and we walked to our units. It was a small air force base and nearby was a small US Army Base, a Vietnamese Army Base, and the Special Forces Headquarters. All of the bases were located fairly close to the South China Sea.

I was fortunate to be stationed in an area near the South China Sea before the fighting, drugs, and corruption gained full momentum. As the war progressed things grew worse for everyone, especially those people living in the countryside. When the North Vietnamese soldiers became involved the war intensified, because they were much better equipped than their allies the Viet Cong. This resulted in many people fleeing their homes and moving to the cities, especially to Saigon.

Vietnam changed during the war. Drugs became readily available and were inexpensive. I once read a person could maintain a heroin habit on $5 a day, which would have cost $200 in the U.S. for the same amount at that time. Graft, a term for political corruption, became more common as did other forms of crime; black market selling, and drug running. The war and after effects, took a toll on the traditional economy of Vietnamese society.

Construction workers or bar staff could make ten times what a civil servant or a Vietnamese Army officer could make. Many middle and working class people in Vietnam made money legally working for Americans. They owned radios, electric rice cookers, fans, refrigerators, stereos, and televisions. These items were a rare commodity. I never saw a television in Nha Trang or on our base during my year tour.

Disease became rampant with Saigon having the highest combined incidence of cholera, smallpox, bubonic plague, and typhoid than any other city in the world. Children had only a one in three chance of living past the age of four. In my experience most of the people looked fairly healthy. I remember only two experiences to the contrary. One was a cleaning maid who worked on base and the other I encountered on the street.

The maid would occasionally bring her ill daughter to work. One day she didn't show up for work and we later learned her daughter had died. The other occurred as I was walking down a street. I came face to face with a young boy who had his hand out seeking donations. Looking down I noticed there was a man with him. Standing only a few feet away, suddenly shock engulfed me, I saw his distorted face and the void where his nose had been. He had leprosy. I only saw this man once, but I will never forget him.

At the Air Force base, people were constantly coming and going, so most of our learning was from the guys who were there awhile. I was an enlisted man at a small base, so I ended up with many jobs during my one year tour. My assigned job was to keep track of equipment around the base, save money and reduce equipment loss.

For example, it was common practice for various units to trade things to each other. Oftentimes the unit that traded the equipment would report it destroyed or stolen and request a replacement. I had to have one member from each unit sign and be responsible for their equipment. I would inventory the equipment and work with a person assigned from each unit to assure the equipment was present and accounted for. If not, we would have to document how and why it was lost.

In addition to my regular job, I was assigned various other jobs as needed. I did various construction projects such as building personnel bunkers, installing steel protection areas for airplanes and outside ground storage areas. I also loaded bags of cement into an archaic large cement mixer. The bags of cement would come up to us on a conveyer belt. At the end of the day, we were so gray with cement that we looked like ghosts. Fortunately, my time loading cement was short lived because they brought in a more modern mechanized system.

Several times, I went on truck convoys to the Air Force and Navy Base at Camh Rahn Bay to pick up equipment to bring back to Nha Trang. My friend Elliot and I always tried to be in the same vehicle. I always sat in the passenger seat with my M 16 rifle. He drove and had the difficult job navigating the narrow and bad roads, and I had the easy part enjoying the scenery. Viet Nam is one of the most beautiful countries I've ever been in. It was only about a thirty mile drive, but it took two hours to get there. When we arrived people with forklifts loaded the trucks while we ate our boxed C-meals for lunch. The trip there and back took all day. We drove past rice paddies, through small villages, and the corner of a rubber plantation.

Now there is a new road connecting the airport in Camh Rahn Bay to Nha Trang. Nha Trang is located on the coast with nice beaches and has become a large resort area with beautiful modern hotels. The airport cannot accommodate large passenger airplanes so they land in Camh Rahn Bay and the new road is used to transport people by vehicle to Nha Trang.

Later I was assigned duty as an auxiliary air policeman providing support for the base. The duty involved an occasional meeting and a trip to the Vietnamese base to shoot M 16 rifles and M 60 machine guns. Afterward we took our M 16s apart and cleaned them before storing them in the Air Police building near our barracks.

Our group was called up only once, but I was on leave in Taiwan visiting my friend Jerry at that time. I was fortunate to leave Vietnam seven months before the TET offensive, which was initiated in the early hours of January 31, 1968. I'm sure the auxiliary unit was called up during the offensive because Nha Trang was one of the places hit the hardest. TET is the New Year's Celebration that takes place in most of the Orient over several days.

Another job I was assigned was to be a truck driver. I spent one entire day in training and didn't even have to prove I could drive a truck. I had only driven a hand full of times the year I was in Vietnam, but they issued me the driver's license which was in both English and Vietnamese (I still have the license.) The streets were bad and I had trouble swerving back and forth fast enough to avoid the many deep holes in the roads. Of course the trucks had no power steering, which didn't help my learning curve. I remember driving on a road next to the South China Sea when my passenger Jim bellowed, "Can't you miss some of the holes?" Despite his desperate plea, we just kept thumping along.

Those were my various duties for the year I spent in Viet Nam. We had a small base, so I was a jack of all trades. I was glad to do whatever asked, because I was what was called a "short-timer." The year was 1967 and I was in Nha Trang Vietnam when I received word that I would be returning to the good ole USA. I had six months to be reassigned before my normal discharge when the Air Force made me an engaging offer.

I was told if I would extend my time to nine months they would assign me to whatever base in the U.S. I wanted. I briefly considered Nellis Air Force Base near Las Vegas, Nevada. But, with a wife I deeply cared for and a son I had never seen, I passed and said, "Hello civilian world! Jennings, Missouri, your boy is coming home!" I was soon discharged and upon boarding the flight, I remember thinking, "I will never see this God forsaken place again."

It was wonderful seeing my son for the first time and holding my wife. All I could think about was living a happy and wonderful life from that point on with my wife and child. Anna Marie and I did have a number of happy years together before our divorce, which I will explain more about later in the book. Life does not always have a fairy tale ending, but I firmly believe, "The Good Lord has always been looking out for me."

I developed some profound personal relationships with some of the guys I met in Viet Nam. I say guys because at that time we did not have women in regular military units. During my whole military career, I saw only a few WAFS (Women's Air Force) at Travis Air Force Base, Tacoma Air Force Base and a few nurses in Viet Nam. Once I got out of the military, I didn't have any more interaction with the guys. Over the years, I have often thought of them. When I drive through Muscogee, Oklahoma I think of my good friend Clinton Kyle who was from there. We were all young then and moved on with our lives when we left Viet Nam, but I think the mutual support and all we shared helped us throughout our lives.

My first wife, Anna Marie, used to say I was not the same person when I returned. I always questioned her response in my mind by asking, "Isn't it normal for a person to change after experiencing a major event like the war in Vietnam?" My year there had pluses and minuses, but I believe overall it made me a much smarter and better person. It's a year I'll always remember in great detail. Recently, I started reading the history of the Vietnam War and have been especially drawn to the personal accounts of American men and woman who served. The stories reveal good experiences that occurred there as well as many terrible events.

For many years I had frequent dreams about being back in Vietnam. In some dreams I was in the military, and in others I was a civilian. There is something about those dreams that can't be explained by reason or common sense. For example, in the dreams I appeared to be happy to be back in Vietnam. Frequently, I would awake not knowing what to think. Vietnam drastically effected my life in a negative way and most definitely had an impact on my job with Mobil Oil. However, I believe the experience also had a positive effect when I became a special education teacher.

My current wife, Joanne, and I traveled to Vietnam in the summer of 2005. This was a few years before it became a popular tourist destination. It took Joanne a lot of time to research, plan, and arrange our trip. I was nervous and did not know what to expect, but I was happy to have made the trip. We spent three weeks on a private tour going from the delta in South Vietnam all the way to the Chinese border in North Vietnam. We visited some of the places where I served in the military and many places I did not see during the war.

One day we flew from Saigon (now Ho Chi Minh City) and landed at Camh Rahn Bay. We met a guide and driver who took us to Nha Trang in a small automobile. We traveled on the new road that was built after the war over the route I had traveled that took some two hours to navigate. The trip took JoAnne and me less than a half hour. When we left Cam Rhan Bay, we got on an odd looking propeller plane to go to DaNang. I told Joanne I had never seen a plane like that. When we landed in DaNang we met out new guide, who told us he was a former South Vietnamese helicopter pilot. I pointed to the airplane and asked him to tell me about it. He told me it was a French cargo plane the French had left in 1954 when they moved out of Viet Nam. The Viet Nam Airline had converted it into a passenger plane. No wonder the aisles were so narrow and the plane looked so odd on the inside and outside. I don't know what year this plane was manufactured, but I'm guessing that it was older than me.

We spent time in Saigon, Tay Ninh, Cu Chi, Myo Tho, Can Tho, Phung Hiep, Soc Trang Nha Trang, Dalat, Hoi An, Hue, Hanoi, Sapa, and Haiphong. It was a deeply moving experience. I found the people in the south generally very friendly toward us and in the north people seemed more reserved, but still cordial.

Many of the people we saw there were born after the war. Others were too young to remember the war. We only encountered one individual who seemed to project negative feelings. Joanne was standing next to me, which blocked the man from my view. We speculated that those feelings might have been due to his experience in the war. She told me that he was glaring at me with what appeared to be hate in his eyes. We speculated that his behavior might have stemmed from his experience during the war. We were in the south at the time. There was no way for us to know his personal situation, but I could understand, even after all these years, why he might harbor resentment. Those were terrible times for both sides fighting in the war.

Joanne said Vietnam was the hottest place she had ever visited. She was right about that, but despite the heat, after our trip to Vietnam I found an inner contentment I can't fully explain. My dreams about returning to Vietnam ceased. Now most of my dreams revolve around returning to school as a teacher. I still have occasional dreams about Mobil Oil even after being gone for two decades. To complicate matters, there are times I have dreams involving both school and Mobil, but don't ask me why.

❦ ❦ ❦

The following are entries to my daily journal chronicling the time Joanne and I spent in Vietnam, which helped bring closure to that chapter of my life.

- **6/5/05**—We met our guide Hugh and driver Fang at 9 a.m. We went to the Presidential Palace in Ho Chi Minh City, which is still called Saigon by most people. We toured the building and outside saw the NVA tank that first crashed through the front gate in 1975. We went to a lacquer factory where Joanne bought six hairpins. Next we went to a dated

French Post Office, an old Catholic Church, two markets, and a Chinese temple. We saw many people riding motor scooters. Some had a man driving with a lady behind him and one or two small children all on the same scooter. There weren't many cars, but lots of busses. At 3:45, we got back to the Renaissance Riverside Hotel, which is located by the river. Our room is on the sixth floor. We went for a swim on the twenty-first floor where the swimming pool is located. Hugh and Fang picked us up at 6:45 to take us to the boat for a dinner cruise down the Saigon River. It was nice not being crowded, having good food, a lively band, and enjoying the cool breeze after a hot day. I took pictures of a few tribal mountain ladies who were working on the boat.

- **6/6/05**—Left at 8 a.m. for the two hour drive to Cu Chi Tunnels, which had been used by the Viet Cong against the French and US. We saw various exhibits: sharpened bamboo traps, rifles, uniforms, bomb making material, bomb with two solider manikins, a US tank that was blown up during the war, a field hospital, and shoe maker. I bought a pair of sandals made from tires for $2.50. These were just like the shoes the Vietnamese soldiers used to wear. We saw the tunnels the Viet Cong used and were able to crawl through one that they had enlarged for tourists. The tunnel was dark, hot, and somewhat scary because I had never been in anything similar. For one dollar a bullet, we could shoot a M16 or AK47 automatic rifle. We passed on shooting, but watched an Australian man. Hugh gave us some hot tea and tasty tapioca topped with crushed peanuts. We drove another hour to the Cao Dai Great Temple and witnessed hundreds of people in various colored robes worshiping during one of their four daily ceremonies. We got back to the hotel mid-afternoon and walked about ten blocks to a five story department store Hugh had told us about. We looked all through the store and I bought conical hats and a Vietnamese doll. Joanne bought dragon and butterfly hairpins. We also bought some food in the grocery section to eat in our room for dinner. We went to bed early.

- **6/8/05**—We left at 7 a.m. and went on a boat to the floating market. Joanne and I were the only white people there. Next we drove to the Khmer People Museum. A little girl came up to us as we were walking out and gave us two beautiful little flowers. In Soc Trang, we visited the Bat Pagoda which is a three hundred year old Buddhist Temple with very large fruit bats sleeping in the trees outside. The Vietnamese people and kids were all very nice us. They were saying hello and were delighted when we took their picture. One girl took a picture of us. Hugh took us to a local restaurant for a good soup lunch. Everyone there, except us, was Vietnamese. They were throwing their empty beer bottles and trash under their tables, but Joanne and I just left our things on the table. We got back to Can Tho about 3 p.m. We decided to walk to a market Hugh had pointed out, but we went the wrong way and got lost. Then we decided to take motorcycles to the market. We paid about one dollar to each driver, but they again took us to the wrong market. We walked around until it started to rain. We took shelter and waited for the rain to ease then took a motorcycle back to our hotel. Even though it was still raining slightly we went to the pool for a refreshing swim and had the pool all to ourselves. We warmed up in the room with a nice hot bath and had apples and peanuts for dinner. We went to bed early and slept well after a full, good day.

- **6/11/05**—Our Sofitel Palace Hotel in Dalat is an old French hotel built in 1910. (The French colonized Vietnam from 1860 to 1945) Our guide Thien picked us up at 9 a.m. and took us to a park where we walked down three hundred steps to a waterfall. Some people were taking photos of a lady and a small girl, both dressed as American Indians. When we arrived, the people wanted a picture of Joanne and me with the lady and girl. We had fun posing and taking pictures of all the other people too. We walked to a large Buddhist Temple overlooking a lake. From there, we took a scenic twenty minute cable ride back to Dalat. We went to Love Park which is kind of a garden area and amusement park. We were the only non-oriental people there. We walked around and later took a forty minute horse carriage ride which only cost $5.00 and I tipped a $1. We went to dinner at a place Thien recommended. Joanne got a regular rice and fish dish and I tried the pigeon dinner. It was alright, but I think I'll stick to southern fried chicken in the future. However, instead of fries I'll order sticky rice so I don't stand out as a new-fangled tourist.

- **6/12/05**—After breakfast, we took a walk to an old, but beautiful Catholic Church. It had stained glass windows with names of the French Catholic people who apparently had paid for them. In the basement were square jars which had pictures on them and inscriptions stating birth and death dates. The jars contained the people's ashes. The French all left in 1954. In the afternoon we drove to Nha Trang. We stopped at the ninth century Cham Tower on the way. It looked like a Hindu structure to me. We checked into the Sunrise Beach Hotel and got a room overlooking the hotel pool and the South China Sea beach. We went swimming in the pool then rested in our room for the rest of the evening. We had some snacks for dinner and made plans for the next day.

- **6/13/05**—It's been many years since I was in Nha Trang, so I wanted to see all I could in a day. We hired a hotel car and driver for the whole morning for just $25. We first went to the old ruined temple I visited in 1966. There were lots of Vietnamese tourists there. The area, which was outside of the city when I was there, now has a lot of houses and buildings. We went to the large Buddha statue, which is over one hundred years old. We saw monks moving in a procession going to the temple. One of the temple guide girls briefly showed us around, then wanted to sell us postcards for 100,000 dong which is about $6. I just gave her 200,000 dong or about $1.25 for a donation. We went to the old Catholic Church on the hill in the city. I visited it in 1967, but never went inside. I was happy when they opened it for us and we got to go in and see how beautiful it was. We drove past my old base, which is now a Vietnamese Army Base. I would have loved to go on the base, but I knew that would not be possible. The other US Army and South Vietnamese bases were gone and are now all civilian housing areas. The old small Nha Trang I knew is long gone. I'm happy I came back to see it because the year I spent there was an important part of my life. We went to the hand embroidery shop, but the ladies who worked there were leaving for lunch on their motor scooters. They looked nice in their brightly colored ao dais dresses. These are traditional elegant Vietnamese dresses cut on the sides and worn over long pants. They are usually made of silk. At noon, the driver took us back to our hotel. We had a quick lunch in our room and then took a walk. We went to a store which sold groceries on the first floor and clothes, pots and pans, household items, and lots of other good stuff on the second floor. It was hot, the store was not air conditioned. Neither floor was very busy, I do not know if it was their lunch hour, but a few of the sales-girls were stretched out behind their counters sleeping on the floor. We bought some water, beer, and food and walked the long way back to our hotel. We changed into our swim suits and went across the street to the South China Sea beach. The traffic was so busy I'm glad the hotel's front guard helped us to cross the street. In the evening, we walked to a German Restaurant run by a German man. Joanne really likes German food, so she was pleasantly surprised. It was a full day which I fully enjoyed. I'm pleased and happy to be back in Nha Trang. I did not recognize much of what I saw, but it's been about forty six years since I was here and time marches on. I was pleased to see that so much progress has been made, and judging from what I observed the people seemed to be doing well.

• **6/17/05**—We are staying at the Morin Hotel in Hue. We left at 8 a.m. for a boat trip up the Perfume River to a large ancient pagoda and two mausoleums of former emper- ors. We were the only passengers. A young lady was selling pictures, statues, clothes, post cards, and drinks includ- ing wine. Joanne bought two rooster pictures and a black blouse for $11. When we got off the boat, we had lunch then spent the afternoon at the Imperial Citadel and our guide showed us where seventy percent had been destroyed by artillery fire in the Hue TET battle in 1968. There were some empty fields because the debris was cleared away, but we did see some partial walls that were still standing. The front of the citadel is still in good condition. We got back at 4 p.m. and took a long walk. We found an Indian, hole in the wall, restaurant with just a few tables near the sidewalk. We got two dinners to go and ate very good Indian food in our hotel room. It only cost $10 for both.

- **6/19/05**—We are in Hanoi. We went to Ho Chi Minh's Mausoleum. After waiting in a long line, we walked past his preserved body which was guarded by soldiers dressed in white uniforms. We walked past a pond through pretty gardens to a two room house that sat up on stilts that he had lived in. A nearby building had a kitchen with medical facilities. After lunch, our guide took us to the Army Museum. Outside we saw a large pile of airplane parts taken from US planes that were shot down. We saw a Russian built MiG Fighter Airplane that we were told was used by nine of the North Vietnamese pilots to shoot down fourteen US planes. I found this hard to believe, but I just nodded my head and kept my mouth shut. We saw different sections of the museum but did not see the section devoted to the US involvement. Our guide told us we did not have time, but we think he didn't want us to see the anti-American exhibits. He asked if we wanted to see a B52 bomber that was shot down. We said yes, so he took us to a place in the middle of the city. Most of the plane was gone. I assume the metal was recycled. What was left of the plane was in a pond of water with houses around it. I believe the plane crashed among houses and the deep indention resulted in rain water forming a pond. We got back to the Melia Hotel about 6 p.m. From our room, we saw a long building with a metal top so we walked there, it was a market with a lot of vendor stalls selling produce, live chickens, meat, tofu, and prepared foods. We bought some mangos. We had a gourmet dinner of crackers, cheese, nuts, and mangos in our hotel room.

- **6/20/05**—We left Hanoi at 9 a.m. for our eleven hour ride to Sapa which is a former French mountain resort. It was a scary ride at times as the driver was going fast and passing on winding roads. There were cows on the road, which our driver went around, but he did hit two chickens. We stopped alongside the road twice for a bathroom break. On the first, Joanne and I took a walk and found a cement ditch, and on the second we went behind a hillside. We got to the Victoria Hotel in Sapa at 8 p.m. We checked into our hotel and then our guide took us to a restaurant. He left us and told us to walk back to the hotel. When we finished, it was dark, we were tired and we got lost. Luckily, we had the hotel card with the name on it so we stopped a few times to ask directions. The people we asked could not speak English, but they pointed and gestured, and we made it back, none the worse for wear, although we were tired after our full day of stimulated travel.

- **6/21/05**—We took a morning walking tour of Sapa and visited a busy market where Hmong and other tribal people set up to buy and sell. Joanne bought a toy flute from a little girl dressed in her native black dress and hat. I bought two bottles of snake wine. Each had a whole snake in the liquid and the sample they gave us tasted more like whiskey than wine. I'll give one bottle to my son Keith and will save the other unopened bottle and put in my display case. We rode back on a motorcycle taxi which was fun. After lunch we walked to an outdoor market area. We saw lots of different products including produce and meat. We saw pig heads and whole beef hind quarters with the hoofs still on them. Joanne has a large bruise on her leg as a result of her fall in the Hmong area. She fell after stepping on a slippery rock.

- **6/25/05**—We are in Hanoi. We rented a car and driver for six hours for $50. We went to the old French prison built in 1895 for political prisoners. We saw guillotines which were actually used by the French. The same prison, which the Americans called the Hanoi Hilton, was utilized by the North Vietnamese to imprison US air crews in the late 1960s and early 70s. We got to go all through the one wing that remained. The rest was torn down to make a hotel and visitor center. We saw the prison offices, cells, shackles, a guard tower, and displays of American uniforms. There were pictures of prisoners and an almond tree that the prisoners had used to make medicine. Next we went to the Hanoi zoo which had a lot of animals from Vietnam. We especially liked the monkeys and birds. Kids were roller skating on a cement ring. We only saw one other Caucasian couple there. They had a young girl with them. We had the driver drop us off at the Thang Long Water Puppet Theatre. Where the puppets were in the water and were colorful and humorous. There was a firework coming from sparklers one of the puppets was holding. At the end of the show, the ten puppeteers who stood in the water came out from behind the curtain. We really enjoyed the show. We took a cab back to our hotel and had dinner there. Our guide picked us up at 8:30 p.m. to take us to the airport for our 11 p.m. Asiana Airline flight back to the US.

CHAPTER 4
LIFE AFTER VIETNAM

WHAT I LEARNED IN THE MILITARY was basically street smarts. I never traveled before I joined the Air Force. No one in my neighborhood even took vacations. During the three and a half years spent in the military I traveled to Texas, California, Vietnam, Thailand, and Taiwan. I went to Bangkok, Thailand, on an R&R (Rest and Restoration) for five days with my good friends, Clinton Kyle and Darnel Fail. A few months later I took a leave for five days to go to Taiwan to see my friend Jerry who was stationed there. I learned to take care of myself and made some wonderful friends while in the military.

It wasn't all peaches and cream though. There were times when I was lonely and scared. I was dirt poor the whole time. I missed my wife and son for a year. After my first year in Sacramento I took leave and returned to Jennings, Missouri, to marry Anna Marie Monaco. I had met her in Jennings through my friend Jerry Rose because she worked with him at Maloney Electric Co in nearby St.

Louis. After we married she lived with me in Sacramento for one year in the state housing project which was located about a mile from the State Capital Building.

We had a kitchen and den downstairs and a bedroom and bathroom upstairs. We furnished it with used furniture which cost a total of about $100. In addition, we purchased a new black and white screen television we bought at Sears on credit. I think it cost about $110 and we paid $10 a month. Our apartment was a nice place and well worth the sixty dollars a month rent, which included utilities.

Several other airman and their families lived in the complex. I remember a couple and their two children from the Fiji Islands lived two doors from us. He was a taxi cab driver. Money being tight, on the last week of the month, I would borrow fifty cents to one dollar from him to get gas for my 56 Chevy until I got paid.

When I went overseas, Anna Marie went back to Jennings to live with her parents. As I previously said, Anna Marie had our first son two months after I left for Vietnam. Our second son Keith was born nine months and one day after I returned home from Vietnam. We did not plan to have Keith that quick, but were both happy that Rob would have a brother close in age. I was ten years old before my first sister was born, so I thought the short age difference would be good for them.

Anna Marie and I didn't have a pot to pee in, but we were positive and knew everything would work out for the best. In other words, we were young and stupid, but luckily in our case, fate did favor the bold. I soon got a job making $2 an hour. It was in a factory job where walls were put together and taken to construction sites for use in homes that were being built. My job was to load the completed walls on a truck using a portable winch like crane. The job was hard and physical, I returned home each day tired and dirty. I would take a shower and a nap before dinner. During my second week, I was loading a wall when I heard a creaking noise. I looked up and saw that the temporary support we put on a wall was bending. I ran just in time to avoid the falling wall which hit the floor right next to me. I decided to quit after completing work that week so I needed to find another job quick.

Anna Marie and her grandmother both previously worked at the Missouri Pacific Railroad headquarters in downtown St. Louis. They suggested I try to get a job there. I bought a plain blue suit for $29.99 and went to the personnel office to apply. The man interviewing me was impressed with my military service, that fact I had a family, and that one of the evening courses I was taking at the University of Missouri at St. Louis was Spanish. He said Spanish would be good to know because the MoPac goes down to the Mexican border. I was hired to work in the Freight Rate Department and completed a ten week training program. I started at $475 a month and worked in the rate quotation section. We would use hundreds of different tariffs to get freight rate quotations or rail routes for customers who mostly telephoned or made a written request.

I did this job for five months until one of the department managers asked me if I would like to transfer to the MoPac owned Texas Pacific Railway in Dallas, Texas. I immediately told him yes because all the Texas guys I knew in the Air Force spoke highly of Dallas. They all had been to the Texas State Fair, which is held in the fall of every year. He told me a manager from the T&P in Dallas would see me the next day. I went home and told Anna Marie about our opportunity. She immediately said, "OK, good." Considering she was more than eight months pregnant, we made a snap decision rather than taking our time to go through a logical thinking process.

I met Don Millender the next day, and we discussed the job that would be a promotion. I would be determining freight rates, which involved working with shippers, other railroads, and various freight bureaus. Mr. Millender offered me the job and asked when I could be in Dallas. I told him I would like to have a month or two. He said, "I need you there by the next week." I agreed and the railroad sent two of their men with a truck to collect our beat up furniture, which they loaded on a railroad piggy back trailer.

Anna Marie and I drove our small car to Dallas with our one and a half year old son Rob. Our younger son Keith was born three weeks later at Methodist Hospital in Dallas. He was a native Texan by a narrow margin. I was now making bigger money, which was about $600 a month. This went a lot further than it did in Missouri because Texas had no state income tax, and costs in general were lower.

About one year after I got out of the military, I used the GI Bill to buy our first house. The small new house had three bedrooms with a two car garage, and it was located on a large corner lot in Irving, Texas. The total cost was $16,750 which was all we could afford then. We got a 6 ¾ % interest mortgage. I had to pay $200 down, which included closing costs and the first month's house payment. It was a new neighborhood, and a new elementary school was located four blocks from our house.

The second blessing was the GI Bill to attend college. I'm not sure if I would have been able to attend college without it. I had started at the St. Louis College of Pharmacy before I went into the military and attended Sacramento City College while at Mather AFB. I also took correspondence courses while in Vietnam. The GI bill helped me get my Associate of Arts degree at El Centro College in downtown Dallas, my BBA degree from Southern Methodist University, and paid for most of the costs for my Master of

Science degree from the University of Dallas in Irving, Texas. I attended evening courses at all of these schools and kept a full time job during the day.

I am giving the reader a lot of detailed information about what happened throughout my life because, as I said in the introduction, I believe everything that happened was leading up to my becoming a special education teacher. For example, if my friend Jerry Rose didn't introduce me to Anna Marie Monaco I wouldn't have married her and later go to the MoPac for a job. If I didn't get the MoPac job I would not have gone to Dallas. If I didn't go to Dallas, I would not have met Joanne Ducotey whom I married. If Mobil Oil didn't put me out to pasture, I would not have become a teacher. It's a long chain of events that led me to becoming a Special Education teacher.

CHAPTER 5
COMING ON BOARD THE DISD

WHEN I STARTED TEACHING in January of 1993, I was approaching my 49th birthday, which was in February. During my whole life I had never given a thought to becoming a teacher. The good Lord really looked out for me when I got the opportunity to become a teacher. Actually, the opportunity was a multistep process which began about four years before.

Over the course of my nineteen year career with Mobil Oil I held several positions. I first started in the transportation department and after five years I went into operation planning in the Dallas accounting center. My next job was as a supervisor in accounts payable before I moved to a staff position in crude oil accounting. My last job was as a supervisor in accounts receivable. It was a fluke that I ended up in accounting and it was the beginning of a seeming downhill journey. However, the journey would eventually lead me to a career field I would love.

Mobil had sponsored a DISD school located in South West Dallas named J. P. Starks Elementary. Mobil volunteers were asked to go one day a week via a company van to the school and tutor one student for an hour. Sadly, no one in our department volunteered. When I told my wife, Joanne, she told me that as a supervisor I should volunteer in order to set an example and lead the way for the others in my section. At the time I didn't really want to sign up, but I am so glad I did.

The first day as we were nearing the school I saw a lot of boarded up apartments and thought, "What did I get myself into?" But once I stepped into the school, I was pleased to see an orderly and clean school with a great principal, teachers and students. I tutored second and third graders for four years until the layoff. I even worked my way up to be the van driver! I could claim that gaining the position was good progress, but the truth was, no one else wanted to drive the van.

There were parts of the job at Mobil I did not like, but I fully intended to stay until I retired because the pay and benefits were excellent. Unfortunately, at the time, there was a major layoff and I was let go. When Mobil started doing the intensive study months before the actual layoff, I sensed I was in big trouble for several reasons. It was rumored my section was going to be moved to another city, I was a middle aged Caucasian man who was lacking in technology skills, and I had already worked my way up the pay scale.

Mobil had also hired a plethora of recent college graduates within the last two years. Most of them were single and did not mind putting in long hours at work. They also knew how to operate and buzz away on a computer. I attended one of the onsite computer classes and sat next to a recent college graduate. He was kind enough to help me during the full day class. The next class I took was about a month later and he was teaching the class. It was plain for me to see that he was headed in the right direction, and I was headed toward the door.

I didn't relish working the long hours, which probably didn't help my cause. For instance, when I was working in Accounts Payable, we always put in long hours in December because of year end closing requirements. Since I was paid a salary many of the people in my section who reported to me made more money than I did because they were paid overtime. I don't begrudge them; it was just the way the system was set up.

A reorganization study was done by various teams. The trendy way of doing that was to tape large posters on the walls that assigned teams could write and draw on. I wasn't on any of the teams so I knew I was in big trouble.

Sure enough, the powers to be, informed me that my whole section consisting of twelve people in Accounts Receivable would be moved to Philadelphia. To rub salt in my wounds, they brought people down from Philly so my employees could train them. They didn't ask me to train the new supervisor; I guess my position was the easiest job to replace. One of the consolidations to my people was a nice luncheon. I was told to take them to a restaurant of their choosing, which I was glad to do. We went to a very nice restaurant and had an enjoyable time. I will never forget the occasion; it was both happy and sad. Several years ago the owner closed the restaurant and the building was torn down. When I drive by the hill where the restaurant was located I still think of our "Last Supper."

Mobil was fair in that they gave me 12 months' severance to be paid out on a monthly basis. They also let me keep my medical benefits for 12 months and paid to send me to a three day seminar that was intended to help me secure a new job. Theoretically, my reward should have been a promotion to the next grade level. If I could have stayed with Mobil until retirement, I would have become a multimillionaire because of the stock plan, increase of the stock's price, stock splits, dividends, and Mobil being bought by Exxon. But, had that been the case, I would have ended up a dead millionaire or at least an alcoholic.

Looking back, I'm happy they told me they no longer had that loving feeling toward me. I was heartbroken at the time. For months whenever I would drive by a Mobil gas station, especially at night when it was lit up, my heart would sink. I was so gung ho when I worked at Mobil that I would only buy Mobil gasoline for my cars and boat. I'm now thankful, because I give myself freedom to buy gasoline from whatever station is convenient-sometimes even Mobil, oh, pardon me; I meant to say Exxon Mobil.

Man, I never thought any company could buy the Mobil Oil Corporation, but I guess there was more than prestige involved. The merger probably came about because of the almighty dollar and the fact many executives were going to be collecting a lot of coins. It appeared to help the stockholders, but from what I've read in the Wall Street Journal for the last twenty five years, the CEO's and Company Officers tend to look out for themselves before looking out for anyone else. Have you read about some of the Golden Parachute deals CEOs receive to leave their companies? Sometimes the parachute deals occur when a company has lost money or when ordinary workers have been burned, but result in the CEO's halo shining a dazzling green or even a brilliant gold. The colors of wealth can go a long way in big business for a select few.

The problem in my case was that I was only promoted twice in my whole nineteen year career. I was moved laterally several times to different supervisor positions while most others were moved with a promotion. Obviously, some of the blame for my non progress rests with me, but I came to believe I was in the wrong place at the wrong time in the very conservative Mobil Accounting Center. Analyzing the events at the time left no doubt that my Vietnam Veteran status had played an indirect role in my being the only supervisor to be let go in the summer of 1992. I did not fit in with my accountant colleagues. Some of the managers would occasionally say, "We're accountants. We're boring, and we want to keep it that way." That was their unofficial motto, but unfortunately for me I just wasn't boring enough for them. I fully agree that I was a different breed of cat.

One other supervisor caught in the downsizing was given a choice to stay, but only if he took a demotion. He chose instead to retire. With an understanding that my experience in Vietnam had played a part in the fact that I was given no option upon leaving, on September 8, 1992 I submitted a proposal to champion Veterans rights.

The following was included in the 1993 Mobil Oil Stockholders meeting. If it had been approved, I would have gone to the stockholder meeting to present and explain:

> My name is Robert H. Anterhaus, and my address is 3817 Alta Vista Lane, Dallas, Texas, 75229. I am a Mobil Oil stockholder. I am submitting the following proposal to be included in the next annual stockholders meeting for their approval. It should be included in the Notice of 1993 Annual Meeting and Proxy Statement. This letter will serve as notification to management that I intend to be presented to the meeting, for action by stockholders, the resolution set forth below:

WHEREAS, Our company is dedicated to fair and equal treatment for all employees, and that company policy reaffirms government regulations forbidding discrimination in recruiting, hiring, training, promotion, and all other terms and conditions of employment on the basis of race, color, religion, sex, age, national origin, citizenship, handicap, or status as a disabled veteran or Vietnam era veteran.

WHEREAS, Mobil Corporation Equal Employment Opportunity Policy states that every good faith effort shall be made to implement affirmative action programs designed to provide equal employment opportunity in all types of jobs and at all levels in the workplace.

WHEREAS, our company has made tremendous progress in the advancement of most minorities. This is rightfully so and good; however it is felt that one minority, namely Vietnam Veterans, have inadvertently been viewed in a somewhat negative manner because of dissimilarities some of them still appear to endure. Because of these perceptions, some Vietnam Veterans have, whether directly or indirectly and intentionally or indirectly and unintentionally, been discriminated against. It is long past time that overlooked minority in our workplace be accorded equal treatment.

WHEREAS, Robert H Anterhaus, Mobil shareholder, Vietnam Veteran (1966 to 1967) and former Mobil employee with almost nineteen years of service, proposes equal opportunity actions for Vietnam Veterans employed by our company be taken. These include:

1. Retain an independent reputable consulting firm to assure Vietnam Veterans are being treated equally. This firm will determine if there are inequalities or legal implications and if necessary, recommend immediate corrective action be taken.

2. Alter present affirmative action programs to include Vietnam Veterans.

3. Assure adequate controls are in place to ensure that Vietnam Veterans are treated equally and in the true spirit of equal employment opportunity policies in both the present and future.

RESOLVED, this shareholder requests the Board of Directors and other shareholders to implement and/or increase activity on each of the Anterhaus Principles.

Mr. Lewis Hering from the Mobil Oil Office of General Council contacted me to let me know that my proposal would be reviewed by Mobil CEO Allen Murray. Mr. Murray would either approve it or not. If he did not approve it, the proposal would be sent to the Securities and Exchange Commission for review. After a few days, Mr. Hering contacted me to say that Mr. Murray had not approved the proposal, but asked if I would like to attend the shareholders meeting. He went on to say that he would be glad to meet with me and discuss the proposal.

It was August of 1992 when I was in the middle of my initiative to champion Veteran's rights when Joanne returned to teaching taking a job as a special education teacher in DISD. She taught severely disabled students in the DISD. Joanne had known from the time she was a little girl that she would be a teacher. She got her teaching degree from Queen's College and her Masters from

City of New York University. She taught in New York City before moving to Dallas and taking a job with the Head Start Program. Joanne had been in the program three years when she had her first child. Wanting to focus on raising her child she transitioned into substitute teaching for the next several years. When we heard the distant thunder at Mobil Oil about a year before I was let go, she made the decision to return to full time.

Shortly after joining the district she learned about a special program, the Dallas Alternative Teachers Certification. The District was going to select college graduates for a ten week intensive program to become teachers. In addition, the program required participants to take twelve college graduate hours in reading, child development, and testing. Joanne suggested I apply.

When I found out about the Alternative Teaching Program, I had only one day to complete the application. I drove to the Alternative Education Center to pick up the paperwork. But, back then, I had no fax or online capabilities to submit the application so I completed the application and took it back the next day. Within two weeks, I was notified that I had an interview. Three people interviewed me. One had a job position in the Alternative Certification (AC) Program, one was a principal, and one was an administrative person. I thought I interviewed well, but I received a letter the next week telling me what a good applicant I was and thanks for interviewing, but no thanks. When I read this letter, it put me in a gloomy mood because I really wanted the opportunity to be a teacher.

The next several weeks I continued looking for a job without any hint of success. One Friday afternoon in September I was sitting on the couch watching TV waiting for Joanne to come home from her teaching job at Cabel Elementary School. When she arrived, I turned off the TV and told her about my frustrating week. I was really in a despondent frame of mind. We talked, and now the only thing I remember was seeing her smile and hearing her say, "So you're a failure, but I still love you." I just burst out laughing. I think that statement put my situation in proper perspective and made me feel much better about facing the future knowing I would never be alone.

The very next Friday it was late afternoon and I was lying in bed faced with another one of my depressed moods thinking about what I could and should do. About 4 p.m. the phone rang, and a lady from the AC Program asked if I would be interested in teaching special education. I told her of course and that special education was my first choice. Upon review, she said that I had marked regular education. I suppose I was in such a hurry to complete the long form that I erroneously marked regular education as my first choice, thus explaining the previous rejection. Fortunately, she arranged another interview for the next Monday, and I was accepted into the program.

The certification program had kept me so busy that I did not take Mr. Hering up on his invitation to meet. Sometimes, I wish I had followed through with my Veterans fight, but life moves on, and I had to do what was best for my family at the time. Now, I know I made the right decision by taking the path to become a teacher. Becoming a special education teacher has been one of the highlights of my life.

Joanne sometimes kindly says, "That Mobil world was never meant for one as beautiful as you." It's very nice of her to say that, but I hold nothing against Mobil and can even smile once a month when my bank receives the small pension I have been collecting from Mobil since I reached fifty five years of age. I wasn't always happy at Mobil, but it definitely served an overall purpose in my life and provided a decent living for me so I could support my family. Now, I'll say, "Thank you, Mobil Oil. We did many good things together, and I will always look back on our union with positive memories."

CHAPTER 6
TEN WEEKS ALTERATIVE EDUCATION PROGRAM

THE ALTERNATIVE CERTIFICATION PROGRAM was established in Texas as part of the 1984 educational reform legislation. It provided an alternative procedure for the training and certifying of high caliber teachers in districts where staffing needs could not be met through conventional teacher education programs. The Dallas Independent School District implemented the program during the 1986-87 school years.

On October 12, 1992, I became the proud participant in the eleventh class or Phase Xl. I arrived at Estes Plaza in Oak Cliff at 7:40 A.M., and the class started on time at 8:00. There were assigned seats so we each found the card with our name among the various tables. Seventy two people were in the class, seven were in the Bilingual Program, twenty in Elementary, sixteen in English as a Second Language, and twenty nine of us in Special Education.

We started with an ice breaker game. The goal was to walk about the room and talk to the other participants in an effort to complete the following list of questions.

1. Who is seeking the same certification as you?

2. Who has on a blue/black suit?

3. Who has dangling earrings?

4. Who was born the same month as you?

5. Who has seen "Last of the Mohicans"?

6. Who has read *Malcolm X* or *Mexico?*

7. Who has been to see the exhibit, "Catherine the Great"?

8. Who has blue eyes?

9. Who speaks a foreign language?

10. Who drives a truck?

11. Who has been married for more than ten years?

12. Who has ridden on the McKinney Street Trolley?

13. Who has run in a marathon?

14. Who has visited a foreign country?

We did this about fifteen to twenty minutes, and then all of us got up and introduced ourselves and briefly told the others something about ourselves. One candidate who was a lawyer told us he wanted to make an honest living. That got a lot of laughs. Another man who recently retired from being a naval officer said he wanted to give back to the community. A young man who was a geologist in the oil industry said he wanted to try another profession. I told them that my oil career had gone south. Not really knowing what else to say, I stretched the truth by saying I had always wanted to be a teacher. Of course, several others had already stated the same, which made it easier for me to claim.

In the early afternoon, we filled out registration and personnel papers. Late in the afternoon was the "Confessions of Interns." Five teachers, all recent graduates of the AC program, returned to speak to our class. They were good, interesting speakers who used humor at times but definitely conveyed the message that it's a very hard job with a small financial reward, but a very rewarding worthwhile career opportunity. I certainly appreciated their honesty, and it gave me a lot to think through.

I realized there was going to be a lot to learn in a relative short time. The days ahead were going to be a long haul with a lot of bumpy roads. So I loaded my internal fuel tank with a load of piss and vinegar and set off for what would become one of the most wonderful adventures of my life!

Upon completing my first day, I had an intense headache. I seriously asked myself if I was going to be able to complete the journey. However, I pulled myself together and determined to try my best. Of course, I didn't see that there was much choice career wise, after being laid off from Mobil; my back was against the wall. The AC Program Director told us as the end of that first day, "Today is the first day of the rest of your life." Her timely statement brought me back to a positive can-do attitude.

For the first three weeks the director had scheduled a variety of different speakers, videos, and classes. Usually we were together as a group, but depending on the daily schedule we sometimes broke up into separate teacher educational groups. This allowed me to get to know everyone, especially the other twenty six Special Education candidates. The first week, several principals come to speak to us and they mostly related what they expected from beginning teachers.

The Preston Hollow Elementary principal said we should show confidence. That we should look people in the eye and give our honest opinions. We should speak respectfully to our colleagues and principal and always be a team player.

The Greiner Middle School principal told us to be honest and professional. He said we should be a role model by not trying to be on the kids' level, but by providing an example for them to aspire to. We should be punctual and show commitment. We should always be fair and treat others equally as we would like to be treated.

The A. Maceo Smith High School principal told us to be articulate and to have vision. He said we must care about students, always look professional and just be ourselves.

The Kramer Elementary School principal told us to go beyond the 8 to 4 work day. He suggested that we should be prepared to do whatever necessary when doing our job. We should get all the training that is provided.

The Lisbon Elementary principal said we should be considerate and flexible. She suggested that we should not criticize others or the school and that we should give children an out, work with them in order to keep their dignity intact. We must always be professional in the way we dress, speak, and carry ourselves. We must have high expectations for our students. She said it was important to talk in plain English to the parents.

The Kramer Elementary principal told us to be positive, caring, congenial, and cooperative. Each teacher must believe that every child in the school is his or hers. We should plan ahead for everything. Be a yes person. Be a volunteer and build relationships.

The principals were exactly to the point in what they wanted from us. I appreciated what they had to say in such an understandable manner. In the fourth, fifth, and sixth weeks, in addition to regular activities, we were to visit their schools and others in the school district and attend various classes.

I learned my first school would be Carter High School and that I would be visiting alone. This caused me some apprehension considering the school had somewhat of a tough reputation. Upon arrival, I met the Principal, Mr. Joseph Brew, who was previously the principal at Walnut Hill Elementary School where my stepdaughter attended. He had done a great job at the Walnut Hill School so meeting him made me feel more at ease. Mr. Brew escorted me around the school for about a half hour and then left me at the resource room where I spent an hour. The next few hours were spent with autistic students. I was privileged to have lunch with them and their teacher. My last hour was spent in the self-contained unit for behavior students. All classes I visited were special education classes.

The time spent at Carter was worthwhile. All classes I visited were special education classes and I only experienced one unusual event. The hall was empty when one of the students was walking me over to the second special education class. However, we came upon a teacher and a student who were having a heated discussion. We knew which one was the teacher because he was wearing a tie. The teacher was more than holding his own against the much taller student who was acting belligerent. After the two of us were well past the pair the student with me said, "That man doesn't back down from no one." Of course, she was referring to the teacher. I would come to understand there would be more to the job than just teaching my special education students. I'll say more about that later.

The other schools I visited were City Park Elementary School, J. W. Ray Elementary School, Samuel High School, Hulsey Middle School, Walnut Hill Elementary School, and E. D. Walker High School. I visited every type of special education unit and learned a lot from the teachers, their assistants, and talking to and working with the students.

I kept a journal during my twenty nine years of teaching. So to give you an idea of what my days were like in the training program, the following are some of the entries during this period.

October 13, 1992: We had a two hour speaker from administration who was very humorous. I ate lunch in my van and read. I had Reading Class from 1 to 2:45 and Advanced Childhood Growth from 3:30 to 5:30. I read again in my van during the afternoon break. We have a lot of reading, plus papers and presentations to do for both classes. The Reading Class is taught by lady PHD from Texas Women's University. I arrived home about 6:15 and watched the vice presidential debate with candidates Gore, Quail, and Stockdale.

October 19, 1992: We had all morning with Dr. Mason. She is really a nice lady who is spending a total of twenty four hours with us on teaching methods. Both afternoon classes went well. We got off ten minutes early to watch the presidential debate with George Bush, Bill Clinton, and Ross Perot.

October 23, 1992: The twenty seven people in our Special Education Program had our first full content day with various special education speakers. Four of these speakers were in the last Alternative Certification Program and are now teaching in middle and high schools. God, it sounds bad, especially teaching middle school emotionally disturbed students. After dinner, I worked on my presentation on Down syndrome for my special education class.

I telephoned my mom to get some information about my brother Joe.

October 29, 1992: This morning we had a guest speaker come to talk to us about children's books. He was interesting and brought nice books for us to look at. It was a tough afternoon. In the first class, I was group leader for twelve of us doing a stage act. In the second class, I was prepared to give my Down syndrome presentation, but Greg who was before me got on a roll with his presentation about black male students in the DISD. He took the whole last hour of class, so I would be rescheduled. I was all ready to do my presentation today, so thanks for nothing Greg.

November 6, 1992: Spent all morning at Ray Elementary School located just north of downtown Dallas. I was in an Early Childhood class with another AC classmate, Joyce. It was a fun morning. We went to breakfast, lunch, and music class with them. We watched them do learning centers, circle learning, and free play. There was one wheelchair boy, two Down syndrome kids, and some hyperactive and some nonverbal students in the class. The teacher was really good. When I got home, I started doing my web and thematic unit paper on the circus. I have to finish it by this weekend for my presentation in reading class.

November 11, 1992: Five of us spent the whole morning in two autism classes at Hulsey Middle School. We learned a lot from the students, teachers, and assistants. We got a good belly laugh when one of the students came over and sat right next to my AC friend Molly. He immediately cut a big loud winder. Molly had a surprised look on her face and didn't know what to do. The teacher made us laugh even more when he looked at the boy and Molly and jokingly said, "Ok whoever did that, please don't do it again." The perplexed look on Molly's face was worth a hundred dollars.

November 16, 1992: I spent all morning at E D Walker Special Education High School in the Daily Living Skills Class. My AC classmate, Michelle, and I were teaching kids how to make biscuits in the apartment kitchen where they have with cooking facilities. In the afternoon, we had student presentations in both classes. They were interesting. I did not have to do a presentation, so I just sat back, relaxed, and learned a lot.

November 19. 1992: I spent all morning in the E D Walker special education workshop for teachers. I made posters, did laminating, and made cutouts. In the afternoon I did my circus thematic unit presentation in the reading class. My visual aids got a lot of good attention. We had a test in our second class. I studied hard, so I think I did well and should get an A.

November 24, 1992: We had special education training this morning, which included two speakers from the TAPS bad behavior unit speak. One lady from the Autism Crises Unit also spoke. For about two hours this afternoon, we had a Thanksgiving party. We all chipped in $5.50 each for a good lunch. We had a talent show. Some of our people sang, played piano, guitar, and the harmonica. We all know each other fairly well by now, so we fully enjoyed ourselves.

December 8, 1992: We had our second day of the two day seminar about discipline management. It's put on by a private firm which Dr. Ingram told us is very expensive. It was very intensive, and I learned a lot. I'm so glad I didn't get picked for some of the role playing activities. Our instructor told a humorous story. She told us that the girls in a high school were putting lipstick lip marks on mirrors and walls in the girls' restroom. The lady custodian waited until several girls were in the restroom then soaked her cleaning rag in the toilet to clean off the marks. She dipped the cloth into the toilet each time she cleaned one of the lipstick marks off. The girls' eyes got bigger and bigger. The word got around fast and there were no more lipstick marks in the girls' restroom after that.

I did not put this in my notes but now I think that the clever custodian solved the problem without saying a single word. I think a person with such great communication skills should get into politics or even better become a school superintendent, but she was much too talented to waste any time being a school administrator. Sorry, but I couldn't resist jokingly saying that about my administrator friends. I hope we can all be honest and at times even joke, especially about ourselves, so we can learn to better work together to help our students. I think communication between education professions will be the easier part. The difficult area is overcoming politics, financial decisions, ridiculous laws, administration hurdles, and whatever other obstacles Uncle Sam or state governments present.

December 17, 1992: It was our last day of class. Yesterday afternoon the program administrator told me that they needed my Master's Degree transcript, so I made arrangements to be at the University of Dallas at 7:30 this morning to get a copy. I got there early, so I walked around the campus, which brought back memories of a tough but good two years of evening classes there. In the morning, personnel gave us a workshop on benefits, safety, and sexual harassment. At 2:30, we had our final party being together as a group. We had refreshments, wished each other well, and had a few laughs. At the end we sang, held hands, and made a big circle shaking all seventy two students and four of the staffs' hands. We sang two inspirational songs, "Tomorrow" and "Well done."

I did not write any more details about the party in my notes and I do not remember the words to the songs, but I do remember how happy everyone was. At that point, we were optimistic and proud we had finished this portion of the training. Surely, all of us were much too happy to be scared. Fear, of course, would come later for many, including myself. For me, it was a dumb fear birthed out of the times where I just didn't know what was going on. The unknown scared me because I didn't want to do anything that would prohibit me making it through the program; especially so soon in the training. Some were not going to make it as teachers, but I think at the time of the party, all felt pretty good about what they had accomplished thus far. We were giving our best shot at becoming teachers. Of course, teaching, as with every other thing in life, has its ups and downs. Reflecting back, I think that no matter whatever happened later, everyone became a better person for the experience.

During the ten weeks we had to do two individual presentations. As we read in my journal, the first presentation I did was a thematic unit to all 72 students in our reading class. I choose the circus and enjoyed reading and researching the topic. I always enjoyed circuses as a child and took my sons annually to the circus in Dallas. Once on a business trip, when I worked for Mobil Oil, I visited and thoroughly enjoyed the circus museum in San Antonio. Relating as such, I ended my presentation with, "May all your days be circus days" and then added, "As future teachers, you've got a hell of a lot of circus days ahead of you!" Oh, how right I was. Now I liken my time in the DISD to a three ring circus, where I had front row seats. The experience was indeed exciting and wonderful filled with many happy memories. I wouldn't trade them for anything.

My second presentation was in our special education class. I spoke about my brother Joe who was Down syndrome and died three days before I married my second wife, Joanne. I also spoke about my step children Warren, who is disabled, and was ten years old and Janice, who was eight years old when we married. They were always such good and lovable kids. Today they are both decent, responsible adults, and I am still glad to be their stepdad.

Warren is a custodian at Alliance Data Corporation. It's a very good company that provides full support to help Warren do a reliable job despite his disabilities. Janice has a doctor's degree in Pharmacy and works in a hospital. I am proud of them both as well as my two sons. Rob was a US Marine F18 fighter pilot and is now doing web design for computer systems. He has a daughter in grade school. Keith has his own tile and wood flooring installation business. He has a daughter who recently graduated from the University of Texas and a son who recently graduated from high school.

All my fellow students were required to give presentations and I enjoyed and learned from each. In the following paragraphs, I summarize some of the presentations which impacted me the most.

Gay spoke about the latch key kids, those who return to an empty home after school, because their parents can't afford day-care. She related how many of the parents feel guilty sending their kids off to school alone only to have them return from school where they spend considerable time alone until they return from work. The children might watch improper cable shows on TV or get into accidents. Being alone at home often resulted in students lacking respect for authority, coming to school tardy, not being properly dressed, and sometimes without their homework. Gay said that possible solutions could be flextime, year round schools, or more affordable day care programs. She discussed some possible YMCA programs.

Henry's presentation was on the disease, Lupus, which is an inflammatory disease that attacks the body's immune system. As a result of the weakened immune system, the disease destroys the body's healthy tissues. It strikes three times as many blacks as whites in the US and mostly affects women. The disease can start between the ages of fifteen to forty and manifests with rashes, swollen joints, or fever resulting in inflammation, pain, and damage to other parts of the body. Henry instructed us that Lupus was not contagious and that medicines were available. However, he cautioned that the medication could cause side effects, such as water retention, weight gain, or fatigue.

Heather's presentation was about ADHD or Attention Deficit Hyperactive Disorder in children. The disorder was discovered and named as such in 1980. Prior to this time, children affected, were viewed as having various behavior problems. Chemicals in the brain cause the disability and ADHD affects more than 5% of children. With some the disorder continues well into their adult years. ADHD interferes with a person's ability to pay attention, so a teacher must be prepared to repeat instructions. Heather closed her presentation relating that a medication named Ritalin was recently being given to ADHD children and had met with some success.

Jaline spoke about classroom management. How maintaining classroom discipline is one of the most important aspects to assure student learning. She suggested having the rules and consequences posted to be sure students understood what was to be expected from the first day of the school year. She let us know as teachers we should be comfortable in advance with the consequences that would be given for breaking those rules. Of course, she encouraged us to reward students with a special treat or verbal praise for the correct behavior. We were also encouraged to include parental involvement when appropriate. A teacher/parent conference was suggested as one form of parental involvement. The conferences would prove even more beneficial for the disruptive students because the child needed to understand that the teacher and parents were working together to benefit the children.

Dennis did his presentation about Dyslexia or Development Reading Disorder (DRD), which frequently runs in families. Dyslexia is a disorder that occurs when the brain does not process letters correctly when reading. Most people with DRD experience low self-esteem due to their inability to read, but have normal intelligence. Interesting enough, in many cases, they have a higher level of intelligence than other people. We learned that the DISD had a Montessori School which was successful in teaching DRD students. The school provided extra learning assistance with individual private tutoring. Dennis said that efforts should be made to recognize Dyslexia early, so that work could be started with the student as soon as possible. He stated that his research showed more boys than girls contracted DRD and that it's better if teachers have their students use cursive when writing. That small letters should be used first and even air writing could be used beneficially.

Lorraine's presentation was on prenatal care. Today much more is known about the mothers' prenatal care than in our grandparents' times. For example, the importance of exercise is vital to the mothers' health. But, in our grandparents' times, they stressed the importance of relaxing and avoiding unnecessary exercise. She reminded us how everyone had smoked in the past, but over time we have learned that the mother should not smoke cigarettes during pregnancy. Among other hazards, smoking can result in babies being born weighing less than five pounds. She also said that drug related births were occurring more each year in our country, especially the use of street drugs, which were extremely dangerous in the first three months of pregnancy. Her research showed there had been over 100,000 cocaine babies born the previous year in the US.

Bonita's presentation was about crack babies. Crack baby is a term used to describe a child, who in the fetal stage, had been exposed to a mother who was smoking cocaine. Most people were aware that addicts sniffed or main lined the drug, but few knew that a stronger high resulted in smoking the cocaine. Her research showed that during the 1980s, crack cocaine had surfaced as a major concern in our country. Crack babies experienced problems with language, behavior, development, and attention. Many woman using crack cocaine delivered prematurely, which resulted in babies weighing less than normal at birth. These babies faced compounded problems because the mothers had poor diets, limited or no prenatal care, some had sexually transmitted diseases, and were using alcohol or other illegal drugs. The financial costs were rapidly increasing. The previous year New York State alone had spent 765 million dollars on crack babies and this figure did not include hospital costs.

Molly discussed fetal alcohol syndrome. When the mother uses alcohol during pregnancy, the alcohol is passed along to the developing fetus. Consuming alcohol during pregnancy can have a negative effect on the baby's physical and/or mental development and oftentimes cause extreme emotional issues, which might result in social consequences. The syndrome caused is especially harmful during the first three months of pregnancy. When the mother drinks alcohol, and especially when she binge drinks, the following complications can develop: miscarriage, heart defects, mental retardation, and problems in the structure of the head and facial features. Later effects for the child might result in bad behavior, delayed cognitive skills, speech disabilities, or negative social skills. Molly suggested a five step approach using a support team to help mothers who use alcohol:

1. Enroll these mothers as soon as possible in a help program.

2. Develop appropriate activities for each mother to assist her to avoid alcohol usage.

3. Teach mothers what is happening and how the baby will be affected.

4. Continued evaluation and testing for both mother and baby.

5. Re-teaching and assuring that that the mother fully understands everything that is involved for both her and her baby's welfare.

Other presentations were on the topics of students' hearing problems, Down syndrome, mental retardation, speech and language disorders, and homeless children.

Please bear in mind that these presentations were summaries of the individual's research on the various topics. Much has changed in the twenty years since I've heard these presentations. Fortunately, in our present health systems, we have more of a vast wealth of information about all the areas discussed.

The ten week training session of the Alternative Teacher Certification Program covered the period from October 12, 1992 to December 17, 1992. All 27 of us had completed the required ten weeks, but later I found it interesting to learn the career status of some of the various AC candidates. The lawyer became a successful middle school teacher and spent many years in the district. The navy man did not make it through the first year, and the geologist soon went back to the oil patch. I likened our class roster to a war casualty list because not everyone was cut out to be a teacher. I'm thankful to God that I lasted nineteen years and ten weeks and was a damn good Special Education teacher in three different grade schools.

Of course, I had no idea what type unit or what school I would be assigned to. It could have been any type of special education unit in grade school, middle school, or high school. Wednesday, November 11th was Veteran's Day, but for us, it was a normal training day, plus we had a job fair scheduled for that evening from 5:30 to 8:00 p.m. Several of the school principals were coming to interview us. No one was aware of the interview selection process and I was confused when I was not asked to interview. However, the good Lord was looking out for me once again.

Lannet who had become my close friend was asked to interview for an autistic unit at the Walnut Hill Elementary School. When she returned from the interview she told me she was not interested, so I asked our director, Dr. Nell Ingram, if I could interview for the position. The director asked the principal, Ms. Judy Zimney, and she said she would be more than happy to interview me. We hit it off and had a good conversation. I shared about my brother who had Down syndrome and my stepson who was in Special Education in the DISD. She told me that she thought my family experience would help me to empathize with the parents. After our thirty minute conversation she invited me to visit the campus and autism unit at the school. I accepted and the following Friday spent all day with the class. I also visited two other autism classes at Walnut Hill and met the teachers and assistants.

On the next Monday, I had an interview with Virginia Nelson who was the director of the Autism Program. She explained that the job at Walnut Hill Elementary School would be like a political football field. Evidently there were some important parents and it was a showcase school for autism. People would come from all over to visit and observe. I told her I could handle the pressure and attention because of my years in business management with Mobil Oil. I related to her about my experience with a disabled brother and stepson. I finished by saying, "My wife is currently teaching severely disabled students in the DISD and will be a good source of information and a sounding board for me." Ms. Nelson said she would recommend me to be hired at Walnut Hill Elementary School.

We often hear what a small world it is we live in. Well, having a stepdaughter who attended Walnut Hill Elementary and the fact that I went to many functions at the school as a parent, was no small coincidence. After I began teaching there, I asked my stepdaughter, Janice, "In your wildest imagination did you ever think I would be a teacher at Walnut Hill Elementary School?" She emphasized every word slowly, "Never in a million years!" I was of the same opinion thinking; life can take some unusual turns. One of the most important aspects in life I learned was to keep getting up when you're knocked down and to keep moving forward. Mark Twain once said, "It's not the size of the dog in the fight, it's the size of the fight in the dog."

To my delight I was assigned to Walnut Hill Elementary School. On December 18, we traveled to our assigned schools to set up our classrooms. Ms. Linda Sievers, taught the older autistic students. I was slated to teach the younger ones. She was selected to be my mentor teacher. The district would pay her a stipend if she agreed and attended mentor training. Her stipend was set somewhere in the range of $500 to $1000 for the year. She accepted the responsibility and over the course of our relationship helped me tremendously, informally and formally. As part of her formal duties she was required to visit my class and write critique reports. I was required to visit her class and write learning reports. She was an excellent autistic teacher and mentor too. I owe a big thanks to Ms. Sievers. She helped me to learn a lot about autistic students at a time when I knew little.

All 27 participants in the AC special education class were required to attend a meeting one evening a week for the first ten weeks of school. We learned by listening to what the other students said and some of the issues they faced. We had two "Super Saturday" classes on February 13th and May 1st from 8 a.m. to 4 p.m. As the time neared for us to take our state board tests to become certified teachers, we had another Saturday class in October. In this last Saturday class, we were given study material, and we spent the day preparing for the special education test. My test was at McArthur High School in Irving, Texas. We started testing in the morning and had all day to finish. I was mentally over the hill, but went over it one more time and then turned the test in. I was sure I had passed.

I got the results several weeks later, 82 percent. My extensive study and test preparation had paid off. I do not know how the others in my AC class did because we were teaching at different schools all over the district. I believe those who did not get at least 70 percent had two more chances to pass the test. In 1993 I received my Special Education Teacher Certification, which meant I could legally teach in any special education field from grade school through high school.

CHAPTER 7
INSIGHTS FROM MY TRAINING

During my alternative certification training, all 72 participants were given a list of 29 tips for a classroom teacher. Both regular education and special education candidates were given the same list. The following are my comments on these from the prospective of my experience in special education. These were invaluable tools I carried with me during my tenure at DISD.

᠁

1. Profit from your mistakes and the mistakes of others.

How very true it is to profit from our past. I had to learn to work slower in some cases, so I could allow myself to think of past mistakes and then act accordingly. It took a while for me to accomplish the discipline, but after a few disastrous events caused by my own actions, I caught on fast. I liken my experience to getting your fingers burned on a hot stove. After being burned for the first time, you approach the hot stove with more caution. The

Committee function at Walnut Hill—posing with our friendly Tyrannosaurus Rex

hard part was to be able to think back and then react within a reasonable time. A teacher has to keep the class and students moving forward without undue interruptions.

Teachers must also observe and learn from the mistakes of others. When practical, it is beneficial to have a discussion about what was observed to find out the details surrounding the event. It is prudent to have another teacher present to gain a better perspective and to not give the appearance you are singling out the teacher. Obviously, it is important that you have a good rapport with the other person.

2. Find things to do without being told.

It seems to me that most teachers keep themselves very busy. Before I started teaching, I thought teaching was an easy 8 to 3 job that required grading some papers in the evening at home. I found out quickly how wrong I was. The reality quickly set in that teaching was tough work. Over the years, I have known teachers who occasionally would stay at school until the custodians closed up at 9:00 p.m. to finish their work. My encouragement to any teacher is to search out and work on tasks without waiting to be told. This will lead to a much more fulfilling career as a teacher.

Every school requires teachers to serve on committees. The committee meetings are mostly held at the end of the school day and sometimes involve school related evening events. Normally there are four or more members of the staff on each committee, and each person has to serve on two, three, or even more committees. Some teachers enjoy the committees because they feel they are helping the school and are involved in the decision making while others feel there are more important things they could be doing with their time.

In my opinion, some of these committees are constructive. One positive aspect I always enjoyed was getting to know the other committee members. Some committees appeared to be just window dressing held for show because traditionally they always existed. All school districts are guilty of having some committees that don't serve the greater good. For this reason I will go easy with my comments about DISD except to say there's a great deal of time that could be better utilized with the students. It is best to be proactive on these committees and make the best of the time spent.

3. Keep your personal life apart from your teaching.

In special education, especially in resource and inclusion, I did not agree that a teacher should fully separate his or her personal life from their teaching. Working with autistic students separating the two was not difficult, but in resource and inclusion often the student needed an honest and caring adult that they could trust and relate to on several different levels.

For example, when we were studying Egypt, I shared the various learning adventures my wife and I had experienced on out trip there. When the discussion of dogs came up, I showed the students pictures of my Border collie named Bippy, who had been a member of our family for fifteen years. I think the key here is to know each student, his or her needs, and how to help them make progress both academically and personally. Students know when a teacher really cares about them.

I also witnessed regular education teachers who successfully used events in their personal life as teaching examples. Thus, maybe number 3 on the list was meant to deal with more mature situations that might occur in some older and higher level academic classes.

4. Plan carefully. First in terms of make ready—prepare materials prior to the day you intend to use them.

Yes, it is wise to plan carefully and to remember how to improve on those plans as time goes on. In my class, part of the planning process involved getting supplemental materials. If students showed an interest in some specific learning tool, I would incorporate it into my next plan. I would key in on that tool more than others. By looking for ways to improve, I was able to gain greater insight into the overall planning process and how to incorporate similar or different activities and lessons.

It was my experience that the special education teachers could be more liberal in planning than the regular education teachers. Regular teacher lesson plans are set to specific common standards, which are complicated to adhere to and rely less on creativity.

Teaching has gotten harder and is becoming more difficult due to the new "super-duper" lesson plans being structurally designed by administrators and politicians. These requirements place the burden on the teacher. They are the ones who spend hours each week compiling the weekly lesson plan based on the design criteria. For example, one of the latest requirements is to send a weekly newsletter to parents. One can imagine how much time is required to send out a meaningful newsletter every week.

5. **Have your materials ready—prepare materials prior to the day you intend to use them.**

Point 5 mirrors point 4, which is necessary for all teachers. In special education, it is not always possible or sometimes desirable to have all materials ready. It is better to know the location where everything is kept so the teacher can quickly adapt. Sometimes it is easier said than done, so it's important to inventory all the academic material from time to time to know exactly what is on hand and where it is in order to get to it fast. The longer a person teaches the more they accumulate material. Personally, at the beginning and end of each year, I would clear out the excess by giving material I no longer wanted to use to students or other teachers. It is my experience that all teachers love to pick up surplus treasures.

6. **Be enthusiastic and show it.**

I think most teachers are naturally enthusiastic and do a good job showing it. However, there are times, especially in special education, when a teacher needs the freedom to show other emotions other than enthusiasm, especially when dealing with a difficult situation involving one of the students. When dealing with the parents it is extremely important not to be overly enthusiastic but to be honest in a diplomatic manner. Exercising honest diplomacy positively worked for me over the long run with the parents. I also appreciated the times when the parent was being honest with me. Two way open communication, benefits the student in many ways, because teacher and parent were working together thinking only of each student's best interest and progress.

7. Get each period off to a good start.

I agree and it is especially true with special education teachers. Teachers should be intentional when considering how to approach each individual student in order for them to get off to a good start each day.

For example, I had one autistic boy who didn't like riding the school bus. He would throw one or both shoes out a window on the way to school. Obviously, the activity was not starting the school day on a positive note. Upon consulting with his parents we learned he loved house slippers, so we spoke to bus management and offered a simple solution; the student would be allowed to wear a pair of his favorite house slippers to school. We then kept his regular shoes at school. For the remainder of the school year he had a good start to each day and interestingly the next year he was okay wearing normal shoes on the bus.

Another boy was always sleepy because he stayed up late each night. We responded by letting him doze off on a bean bag chair until the class left for breakfast. The twenty to thirty minute rest was all he needed to get a good start on the day.

Personally, I didn't have a problem getting each period off to a good start. In my autism class I used the picture communication system. Students were given a picture with a word on it for each activity, and we would tell the student to check their schedule. When I taught resource and inclusion, I followed the general education teacher's instructions. If the resource and inclusion was to be held in my classroom, I always picked the student up and took then took them back to their regular classroom. I would work with one to four students at a time, so it was easier for me to keep their attention, much more so than it was for the regular education teachers who had fifteen to twenty and sometimes more students in their class.

8. Use the pupil's ideas as well as your own.

It is amazing how street smart the students are. I think they are far ahead of us when we were students at their age. I found that students can learn from each other and can constructively continue to build on another student's comments or ideas. When I was in the regular classrooms, I noticed the regular education teachers drawing out thoughts and ideas by breaking the class up into small groups consisting of two, three, or four students in each group. The teacher then might monitor each group or let the group work by itself and present its work to the whole class for discussion.

9. Keep your sense of humor.

I fully agree that a sense of humor is vitally important in special education. It must be natural, constructive, and not in any way downgrading to anyone. At the same time, it must be controlled so that the class does not get distracted and off task. I believe injecting humor is harder for the regular education teachers than it is for the special education teachers. I always admired and respected them and truthfully didn't know if I could do their job on a daily basis. Of course the reverse is true, over the years, I've had a few of the regular teachers tell me that they could not do my job. I think as professional educators, it is important to find your niche where you can best serve the students.

10. Keep the attention of the group centered on the class activity.

Maintaining student's attention is extremely important to the learning process. My assistants were a big help, especially when therapists were scheduled to work with our students.

In my autism classes, there were of course times when I did not have the full attention of all students. During these times I quickly adapted to get their attention. Yet at other times it was more effective to keep the class moving and let the person dream on providing they were not disturbing the others in class. Again the key was knowing when and how to adapt.

11. Say so if you do not know the answer. Then find out.

I have always been comfortable letting students know I don't have all the answers, but that I knew how to find them. This actually happened quite often since the student curriculum is so much more advanced than in years past. The pace of learning is also more rapid. When I didn't have an answer, I would make a note to myself, so I could go back later and research the needed information. Thus, I made it a point each day to wear a shirt with front pockets where I had easy access to pen and note paper.

The information I researched provided a learning experience for myself and the students. These times presented another win-win opportunity for the students and me. By modeling the behavior is was able to encourage students to practice honesty when faced with a situation where they didn't know the answer. You will find modeling this behavior to be one of the most relevant when teaching.

12. Help your pupils to see relationships in, and applications of, their learning.

I agree and hope teachers reading point 12 really understand without further definition the importance of the practice.

For example, I was tutoring an afterschool program made up of regular education third and fourth graders. I asked for volunteers to tell me what their parents' jobs were. The first child told me his dad installed sheetrock walls. So we discussed how his dad had to measure the opening, then measure the board in feet, inches, and sometimes fractions of inches before cutting to make sure when installed there was a correct fit. The second girl said her mother made cakes and pastries at a super market. We discussed how her mother had to follow a recipe and measure flour, sugar, and the other ingredients in cups, ounces, or teaspoons. She would then mix everything together and bake at the correct temperature for the time required. There were approximately eight students in attendance that afternoon and all had an opportunity to share with the class what their parents' occupations were. Our discussion focused on how each of their parents used math learning and applications in doing their job. The students all seemed to enjoy and learn from the practical application learned during the session.

13. Try to keep all pupils interested in the activity and discussion.

Keeping them active in discussion of an activity was especially relevant when I was teaching my autistic students. With the range of interests being so varied, I experimented with work tasks and activities they enjoyed doing. Therefore, they were more inclined to participate, which helped their learning process and often brought about better behavior.

14. Make provisions for the rest of the group while you are working with and individual pupil.

I was very fortunate to have excellent assistants. They knew how to work well with the students, and we worked closely together for everyone's benefit. I frequently asked for their input, and they knew they could say what they thought to me, even without my asking. I would like to thank my assistants and say that I share my success over the years with them. I had no male assistants. All of my assistants were ladies, and I consider them to be like my own sisters.

15. Make full use of instructional aides and remember community resources.

A few of the autism workshops taught us how to make work tasks using common things like egg cartons, coffee cans, different cardboards, and so forth. I did make a few of these items, but personally I preferred to go to garage sales and purchase things I could customize to use for the various students. My wife and I would go most Saturday mornings and then do our grocery shopping later.

When I was in autism, funding was either feast or famine. The various times when we did receive grant money my challenge was to use the funds wisely. I made sure to purchase the best items to facilitate student learning at the best price. In earlier years, we could buy whatever we wanted at most any place. One of my most successful purchases was an old hard wood children's rocking chair I found at a flea market. I got the lady to write me a receipt, which was all the district required from me in order to get reimbursement.

Later in my career we had to use specific forms for reimbursement and could only provide items for the students from established businesses. The idea was to eliminate fraud, but it also limited our purchasing power and innovative ideas as well as making the items much more expensive.

One of our most successful community projects we started at Tom Gooch and introduced at Ben Milam occurred at Christmas. Of course in the DISD we were not supposed to use the word Christmas because it is considered a religious term. Instead we were required to say winter break. We held a party in conjunction with the Wheelchair American Veterans. We provided a list of the best and most fun learning items for each student, and the veterans bought the presents for each student. The Veterans would visit the school on a day during the last week before the break. We'd send the gifts home with the students so they could use them over the two week break. The party was a fun time had by all.

16. Stay away from excessive use of stereotype expressions such as "OK," all right," etc.

Personally I had a challenge with 16 because I would rather speak in a common language the student could understand and relate to. This facilitated constructive learning and allowed us to keep the class moving. Of course, please note, I am not referring to hip or street jargon.

17. Be sure the lighting and ventilation are the best possible in the room.

Yes, when it's possible. In most of the schools I taught in, some rooms were hotter or colder than the rest. Lighting was always good, and ventilation never seemed to be a problem for me. In a few of the very old schools, mold was a big problem. When my wife was teaching at City Park her classroom was located in the basement. When there was a heavy rain the area would flood and mold became a serious concern.

I always kept tools in my classroom to make simple repairs. It is my guess keeping your own tools is probably prohibited today. But, if you are allowed, there are times it will be much faster to fix minor issues yourself than filling out the required job request forms and then waiting days for someone to make the repair. I remember one evening after school at Walnut Hill I fixed the toilet located in a small room behind my classroom. I had done the repair many times at home, so I figured why not fix it myself at school.

18. Give the pupils a chance to discuss, answer questions, perform the demonstrations, etc.

One would assume it would be obvious to engage the student, but I guess it's a good point to mention for new teachers. I think the hard part for new teachers is how to learn when to initiate these activities, how to control the class in its progression, and how to keep the class moving on with the planned lesson without getting bogged down. I believe most seasoned teachers know from experience, how to engage the student while considering their particular interest or advantage with respect to the learning experience.

19. Accent the group—the "we," not "I."

I wish we would have incorporated the concept more sincerely during the many years I was in the business world. It was my experience that a lot of business people used the word "we," but only verbally. They did not model the behavior on a consistent basis, because there was too much money and glory at stake. There were of course many decent business people I knew and worked with that were consistent and thoughtful. However, there were far too many I saw who used the word "we" mostly to help number one. I'm proud and happy to report that myself and my assistants consistently used the word "we" and modeled the behavior as such during my teaching career. Working with nice people who actually used the word as an inclusive term was real pleasure.

20. Move about while talking.

From my experience, moving around applies more to general education than to special education. In our class, it was extremely important for my assistants to be in the best locations at various times during the day, especially during lunch, in school assemblies, or out on the playground. I seldom had to communicate as such, because we all knew positioning was important to keep the class and other activities flowing. I was fortunate to have professionals who worked hard, planned ahead, and knew and loved our students.

21. Try to get variation into the tone and volume of your voice.

I think this statement would be true in most businesses. The key point is to be sincere, honest, and caring.

I learned about voice tone and volume in the Dale Carnegie course I took in 1989. I wasn't really too keen on taking this course, but I knew I wasn't setting the corporate world on fire at Mobil Oil. I always tried to improve and do the best job I could at all of my jobs throughout my life, but at that time, I knew I had a long way to go and a short time to get there. I spoke to my boss, in Accounts Payable, Mr. Don Fry, and told him I thought the course would help considering public speaking was one of my weak points. He spoke to his boss, and they agreed that Mobil would pay the $795 tuition for the fourteen week course. I attended every Thursday evening at the Harvey Hotel on Midway Road in Dallas from 6:30 p.m. to 10:00 p.m.

I still have my graduation picture of the twenty nine students, four graduate assistants, and our instructor. Completing the course really helped me to come out of my personal conch shell in regard to public speaking. I still had a lot to learn and was fortunate when I got the opportunity to be a graduate assistant in another Carnegie course in 1990. There were four of us who demonstrated the various talks and assisted the students. Although, we were not paid for being assistants, we benefited by getting another course for free. Not to mention, the added benefit of attending the weekly meetings with the teacher after each class session.

Mobil and I got our money's worth. I should say Mobil got its money's worth, and I got my blood, sweat, and tears worth. When I would get home each Thursday night, I would jokingly tell Joanne, "Your hero is home." The truth of that statement is that actually I felt like a hero because the course was a Herculean effort for me each week. It required a lot of time to prepare and practice for, but the hardest part was when it was my turn to give my presentation. It did get easier, I learned a lot, and I became more comfortable as the weeks went by.

I want to thank Ms. Debbie Leffke for being such a great teacher and for selecting me as one of her graduate assistants in the second course. I also want to thank Mobil Oil for paying the $795.00 tuition. If Mobil had not paid that that tuition, it may have given me an excuse not to take the course. I can't think of any better learning experience available to help in overcoming a sheepish sensation toward public speaking.

I also took a three day Mobil Oil sponsored course at the Zig Ziggler headquarters near Dallas. Only Mobil employees who volunteered could attend. I also represented Mobil Oil as a volunteer speaker for the Dallas United Way at various businesses in the Dallas area for the last three years at Mobil. I much preferred choosing to go on my own rather to be required. Being assigned to attend training courses happened often at Mobil. I assume these "offers you can't refuse" opportunities happen at most organizations.

I think most of my training at Mobil Oil did me little good in the oil patch. But, later I came to the revelation that the courses Mobil forced me to take helped prepare me for a career in teaching. I spent nineteen years at Mobil Oil spinning my wheels, but the next twenty years spent as a teacher, was like driving a super charged race car. It's sometimes strange how things work out in life.

22. Win the respect of your pupils first and their liking you will follow.

I would just like to state that a teacher should be firm but always fair. In my opinion, this statement applies not just to students, but also to other adults including school staff and parents. I think that being genuine is important to everyone in all professions. In our schools winning the respect of students is especially applicable for principals, therapists, and administrators.

I was fortunate because I started my teaching career in my late forties so I had a lot of life experiences behind me. My specific goal was never just to make people like me. I think some did like me because I was open and honest. On the other hand, I think others disliked me for the same reason. As a teacher, I was comfortable just being myself, which wasn't always the case in the business world. I have read many biographies, but the only person I can think of whom everyone liked was Will Rogers from Oklahoma. He was a great writer, actor, humorist, and rope twirler. Our country lost a real hero when Will Rogers was killed in a plane crash in Alaska.

23. Assume responsibilities for the room appearance and bulletin boards.

Over time, I learned how to make the classroom more functional for learning and to better insure safety for my special education students. I always spent a lot of time and effort on our class displays and especially hall bulletin boards. Everyone in the school, parents, and visitors could see and admire these works of art and creativity. I was always proud of my students' work and wanted everyone to know how talented and smart they were. At times, I let the assistants design and work with our students on the displays. Both the assistants and the students enjoyed working together.

Permanent display in my room at Tom Gooch

Hallway bulletin boards

24. Use good taste in dress: care about your appearance.

In special education, I learned to keep another set of clothes in the room or in my car. We were potty training a three year old boy and he was sitting on the toilet when I heard my assistant say, "Oh no, Bob, come in here!" I went into the bathroom and saw that he had a bowel movement and had gotten it all over himself. I briefly stood there thinking what to do and he proceeded to wipe his hand down the front of my shirt. Luckily I had an extra shirt in my gym bag. Before I changed my shirt, we washed him off in a nearby shower and put on his extra set of clothes his mom thankfully had packed in his bag. I learned a lot teaching autism. One of the most important things I learned was not to crowd a student while figuring out my next move. They always seemed to have the next move figured out before me.

25. Watch your speech habits—use correct grammar, good enunciation and pronunciation.

Many new teachers will make mistakes related to speech, but they will learn to do better over time. I will admit I made my share of mistakes. My grammar still suffers at times, because I speak the way I was bought up by my parents and the neighborhood environment I lived in. Neither I nor any of my friends were slated to be lawyers, doctors, or other professional people. If we were lucky, we would turn out to be career military, policemen, plumbers, or construction workers. If we were really fortunate, we would have our own small business. That's the way it was at that time where I lived. A few of us won more in the game of life than we should have considering the cards that we initially were dealt. I myself am thankful to the US military and government for providing me the opportunity to achieve my success.

Yes, it's the same government I criticize for their expensive muddling of our public school system. No one is perfect, so I am sincere when I say, "Thanks, Uncle Sam, for all the good things you did and still do for me and for everyone in our country."

Uncle Sam is not the only culprit that I should point out. School districts are seriously affected by state laws and regulations. Like Texas, which I am most familiar, other states have vast room for improvement concerning their laws and regulations being imposed on their school systems. The testing at the state level is interwoven with federal laws and regulations creating a tangled mish-mash that ends up not necessarily benefitting the students.

26. Watch your spelling.

25 and 26 are akin to each other. I have always made it a point to recheck my spelling, grammar, and punctuation on correspondence. Time did not allow me to spend a considerable amount of time tweaking documents for the parents. When I was in autism, I sent a notebook home with the student every day telling the parents about their students' day. You can imagine the amount of writing that was involved. Over the years, I got much faster at providing the parents only relevant information, thus avoiding the need to spend excessive time auditing what I wrote.

27. Plan carefully in regard to details, such as handling materials, making arrangements in advance, etc.

In regard to teachers, most of the teachers I've observed have done a good job in regard to this statement. The key here is for teachers to use their time as efficiently as possible because of the many distractions and needless non student assignments they must account for. I know many teachers put in much more than forty hours a week. Teaching is not a regular 8 a.m. to 4 p.m. job.

For example, there was a middle age lady who went through the Alternative Certification Program who taught at Ben Milam. After one year, she resigned and went back to her regular job. She told us it was the hardest job she ever had. She genuinely loved the kids so she would come back at times throughout the years and volunteer. She always worked in the class where the students she had taught were and advanced with them from grade to grade.

28. Be proud that you are a teacher.

I don't think I ever met a teacher who wasn't proud of his or her profession. Personally I am more proud of my teaching career than any other job or profession I had. That includes over a half century spent in the military, the railroad industry, cement manufacturing, and the oil industry. I believe I would still be teaching if the downsizing in 2012 had not occurred. Teaching and the students kept me young. It was challenging, but it was also exciting and fun. It kept my mind active much like popcorn kernels being popped in a microwave oven.

29. Be sure to have the attention of the full group before you begin discussion or make announcements.

What a valid statement, but it would help to give teachers more insight how to accomplish the feat.

That was the extent of the classroom tips for teachers. I think we pretty much beat that list to death. With that said I will keep the material moving forward just like I did keeping the activities moving in the classroom.

CHAPTER 8
MY FIRST COMMAND AT WALNUT HILL

IT WAS DECEMBER 1992 when I secured the job at Walnut Hill Elementary School. I spent the holidays working in my classroom and preparing for the new semester that would be starting on January 5th, 1993. I was assigned an assistant, Mrs. Carmen Montes and we were set to begin with six male students ranging in age from three to six years old. I found it interesting that all my students were going to be boys, but later learned that we were in a time period before autism had been redefined and the diagnosis expanded. Ninety percent of all autistic students were male. In March, we received another student named Monty, also male, who had just turned three years old.

That first semester was a real learning experience for me. Each day I arrived at school about 7:00 a.m. and usually left no earlier than 5:30 p.m., determined to learn all I could. I spent the first couple of weeks finishing the set-up of our classroom, constructing learning centers, and getting my lessons in order. I read my students' education folders in order to find out all I could about each student and their history. The former teacher had been a school parent and functioned only as a temporary teacher, but was a good source of information. My assistant had actually participated in the class so she helped educate me on the students as well. Through our numerous conversations and asking a lot of questions I felt I possessed a good overall knowledge of the students.

At the time, teachers did not have computers, so all documentation, report cards, and everything else was done with pen and paper. This actually made the reporting process much easier for me at that time, given my poor computer skills. My assistant, Mrs. Montes, and my wife, who at the time was teaching a severely disabled class at City Park Elementary, were also a tremendous help.

I got sick a few times that first semester from viruses I caught from my students. I learned that contracting disease is fairly common for first time teachers, especially during those months when the weather is real bad.

When I received my first monthly paycheck for $1,303 ($1,547 before deductions and a whole lot less than my checks at Mobil) I was as proud as a peacock in full bloom. I was performing a job that I tremendously enjoyed, thus the amount was more than acceptable.

Walnut Hill Elementary is a small historic school seventy six years old situated in a nice area of North Dallas. The school, known at the time, as an elite school had no children who lived in apartments. The apartments located nearby were situated within the borders of other school zones. I believe all DISD schools were assigned a corporate sponsor and IBM adopted our

First Classroom at Walnut Hill

little elementary school. Folks, with IBM as our sponsor we were blessed with prestige, commitment, and big time money!

Every Tuesday IBM sent some of their people to teach the teachers. I had one such IBM volunteer assigned to work in my class for an hour or two one day a week. She was a college graduate and had earned her teaching degree, but hadn't taught a single day. This, as our experience with her showed, was probably a wise decision on her part. I'm sure she would verify the truth of my claim. Never the less, we accepted her and appreciated her efforts.

On one occasion, IBM paid all expenses for our teachers and assistants to attend a meeting at a hotel in Las Colinas. The agenda called for us to go on Friday evening for a group meeting, stay overnight in the high class hotel, and go home late Saturday afternoon. All the presentations were done in a large conference room by IBM personnel. Some of the veteran teachers were excited to take IBM up on their luxurious offer. Some of the newer teachers saw it as an opportunity to get to know everyone better and a chance to pal around with the principal. I'm sure a dreamer or two felt the event might be their ticket to gain entry into the promised land of employment with IBM. I was the lone eagle when it came to my feelings. I had been through my share of the phony baloney when I was at Mobil Oil so I felt my time would have been better spent in preparation for my students.

Live and let live seemed to be the attitude at the time within DISD, which reminded me of an event when I was in Vietnam, in 1967. We had flown into Ton Son Knut Airfield about nine p.m. and could not leave until the next morning. The base personnel took us to an old, wooden barracks. My friend Clinton Kyle asked if he could take the top bunk near the light so he could read, so I slept on the bottom bunk. In the morning, he told me some rats had been walking across the rafters above his head during the night. Then he said something which I found curious, "Live and let live, as long as the rats don't bother me, I won't bother them."

Guess I just wasn't the type to just live and let live. IBM policy required that two people share a room and I had no desire to bunk up with another person. I didn't mind sharing a barracks, room, tent, or floor with my military buddies, but not with fellow teachers. Instead, I choose to return home on Friday night. Saturday, upon waking, I felt ill and made the decision to stay at home. However, since Saturday was considered a staff development day I was informed that I would have to make up the day at school preparing a report on ADHD students for the principal. So while the other teachers took off on Friday before Easter I remained to endure my punishment.

After my first year, my assistant, Ms. Montes, retired. She was very experienced and knew how to handle children; she had five children of her own. The school had difficulties finding a replacement because it was hard duty, and the pay was low. Thus, I had several assistants over the next two years. Most were substitute teachers and for the most part performed pretty well. However, I did have an issue with one in particular, she was what we called a "mover," a term used within DISD to represent a person who had a problem working with others or who had been involved in a serious issue. The simple solution was to "move" the person to another school.

My "mover" (I know better than to use her real name) was frequently absent, which left seven students for me to tend to by myself. I would eat my lunch in the room and forfeited my planning period. Luckily, being located in a portable building there was a small bathroom. When I had to use the facility, I would do so quickly with my head bobbing partially out the door to be sure everything was okay. One day this particular assistant turned in a report that one of the autistic boys had tripped her. As a result, she was experiencing back problems. Of course, no one including myself saw the event and the boy could not speak for himself.

As it turned out, she had long term disability insurance, so when a cooperative doctor wrote a friendly diagnosis, she was able to go to the house. Hello early retirement! Admittedly, I was not sorry to see her go, but was disgusted that she would receive disability for the rest of her life. The only good that came from her exit was that no other school would have to tolerate her antics. Welcome to the DISD.

It was not just incompetent assistants the District moved, oftentimes they moved unsuitable principals. This was considered standard practice in the DISD at the time and was not going to be easy to change. However, I attended a school board meeting on September 22, 2012 where the members were considering what to do with the excess number of employees in the District. One member on the school board said that they didn't want to terminate teachers, but due to finances didn't see any other option. He compared the District and finances to a car running out of gasoline. The irony here lies in the fact that in the past, we could not get rid of sorry employees, but now we were going to be forced to terminate good, capable teachers. Do you think such reasoning can be considered progress?

To the DISD's credit, they did let go some administrators that needed to move on. Unfortunately, later they brought in upper level administrators at much higher salaries. I guess they justified the hires thinking somehow by paying these people more our budgetary issues would vanish. Personally, I am of the opinion that the number of administrators let go was just a token number. Many more administrators, who don't teach a single student, are still in the District spinning their wheels and burning DISD gas money while many good teachers are hitch hiking trying to find a new job. In no way, shape, or form is the shift in thinking right!

I learned a lot during my two and a half years at the Walnut Hill Elementary School. I taught both autism classes. I spent a year and a half teaching younger kids age three to six and one year with older kids up to age twelve. I am especially proud of my time spent teaching those younger students, many of whom joined my class the day after their third birthday. Being their first time in school proved challenging for them and for me. However, the students and I learned and grew together.

As in life, much of my learning came through the school of hard knocks. I made my share of mistakes, like any new teacher, but more importantly I learned from those mistakes and vowed not to repeat them. One of the many things I always enjoyed about teaching autistic children is that they taught me something every single day. I believe learning is best when flowing between teacher and student. I can honestly say I did the best job I could.

CHAPTER 9
MOVING ON TO TOM GOOCH

A T THE END OF MY FINAL YEAR at Walnut Hill Elementary School, the principal informed me that I would be moving to another school. The decision had been made to move the entire class to Tom Gooch Elementary School. Although I did not know much about the school, in a way I was happy to hear the news. Walnut Hill Elementary was a good school, but they didn't seem to fully appreciate the special education program. My perception of the staff's attitude could be likened to a big time city slicker who had a country bumpkin for a cousin that came to live with him. The arrangement was awkward because they were from two different backgrounds. The staff just didn't seem to look favorably on the special education kids. Keep in mind, the year was 1995, long before special education evolved into today's structure.

Tom Gooch and Walnut Hill schools are similar in some ways. Both are situated in North Dallas, which is one of the nicest areas of the city. Both were small and did not have an assistant principal.

Classroom at Tom Gooch

Both had only three or four portable buildings. However, the main difference between the two schools was the students. Many of the students attending Tom Gooch lived in apartments. There was a Catholic organization sponsoring immigrants in one of the apartment buildings, so at times we had students from Korea, Bosnia, Kurdistan, and other countries.

In the six years I spent teaching at Tom Gooch I had two foreign students, a seven year old from Kurdistan and a girl named Stephanie from an Eastern European country. I also had five permanent female assistants at various times.

The seven year old had only been to school only one day in his home country. Back home in Kurdistan at the end of the boy's first and only day in school when his mother arrived to pick him up, the teacher pointed toward the door and told her not be bring him back. When we conducted his initial ARD (Admission, Review, and Dismissal: called by other names in different states) meeting, one of the administrators attending brought in a translator. We learned the mother was so excited her son was going to attend school.

Even though he had only spent one day in school, he had attended longer than his mother, because she had never gone to school. The main administrator told the mother she would need to spend the first day with her son. I knew immediately we were headed for trouble. With her present that first day the boy ran wild throwing things, grabbing food, and would not listen to anyone including his mother. Of course, the school didn't think to provide a translator for his transition. Fortunately, the mom caught on quickly that with her present he was not going to behave and she returned home.

Once his mother left, I was able to get the boy under control using our Total Communication System. I understood what he needed because of my past experience with students. He was a smart boy and learned rapidly. By the end of the week, he was smiling, following directions, and learning. Unfortunately, because of his disability diagnoses, I lost him after a few weeks. He was sent to another type of class in another school, although Gooch remained his home school. I hated losing that boy. Children left frequently for the same reason over the years and others left because parents were relocating or the student was being moved up to middle school.

Stephanie had an American mother who had gone to the country in Eastern Europe to do volunteer work in an orphanage. She adopted Stephanie and brought her back to the states. Stephanie was fairly small, but in some ways the toughest student I ever had. There were times when she would quickly try to hurt herself or others. She mostly tried to bite or head butt the adults. Occasionally she would scratch or hit herself. We had to keep an assistant just for her. At times, it took three of us to calm her. Her program called for us to place beanbags under and on top of her or to use an elastic rubberized type four inch wide tape to wrap her from shoulder to waist keeping her arms inside. She knew when she was about to lose control. Since she couldn't speak, when she wanted to be wrapped, she would go to the shelf where we kept the tape, nod her head, and make a verbal sound. Over time, Stephanie made slow but steady progress. I had her in my class for several years until she moved to middle school.

One of my assistants was a lady named Belki, who had recently arrived from Cuba and could not speak much English. However, she was a fast learner and soon picked up the language. She had been a nurse in Cuba, was smart, caring, and strong. Belki was not much taller than Stephanie, but she was dedicated, so I assigned her to be a one-on-one with Stephanie. The two of them formed a good rapport and Belki even helped Stephanie's mother at home on the weekends.

Two other assistants were Sharon and Dicloria. Sharon was a one-on-one assistant with one of our students, and Dicloria was my class assistant. They were both tough, but loving. I felt bad for Dicloria when one of the students bit her. I bet she still has a scar on her arm.

It was not unusual for a student to try and bite another student or a teacher. Mostly the children just ignored each other except when they wanted someone's food, toy, or other item. I was bit once on the arm trying to help a boy do his work task. The boy's action was really more my fault than his. It was late on a Friday afternoon right before spring break. I was pushing him to complete his work and made the mistake of standing rather than sitting next to him. This intimidated him so feeling pressured, he bit me. He was the first and last to bite me, although others tried.

Another assistant was also assigned as a one-on-one with Stephanie for a period of time. Unfortunately she developed cervical cancer and we would let her rest when she needed to. We were devastated when she went on leave and passed away. Over the years I saw some very tragic things occur, but I also saw many inspiring and wonderful events.

My last assistant at Gooch was Barbara, who was also from Cuba and had to learn English. She did such a great job that when I was being transferred to my next school I asked if she could be moved with me.

All of these assistants were exceptional. I only had one assistant during my years of teaching who didn't meet expectation. I also had eight principals who were all good except one who never should have been promoted. I won't go into much detail about her, but will share one story. The first time she addressed the faculty as a principal she said, "It's about time I was promoted. I have been an assistant principal for eleven years and was beginning to wonder who I pissed off." Guess someone knew for eleven years that she wasn't cut out for the head job. Fortunately, the DISD is doing a much better job in appointing principals. Years ago selecting principals was like playing political football, sort of a "hit or miss" process. Welcome to the DISD.

After being at Tom Gooch Elementary School for four years, I was becoming a very good teacher. In fact I won "Teacher of the Year" for the 1998-1999 school year. In the first round of voting, all teachers secretly cast their vote for one teacher on the staff. Once the votes were tallied we learned there was a tie between myself and another long time teacher. In the second round of voting I received the most votes and was named Teacher of the Year.

I had no idea what duties were required for the Teacher of the Year, but I soon found out. I was required to attend a special breakfast, events with my Principal, and was required to complete the following: Professional Biography, Educational History, Professional Development, Community Involvement, Philosophy of

Teaching, Educational Issues and Trends, my views on the Teaching Profession, and what my message would be if I became State Teacher of the Year.

The following is an excerpt from my diary dated May 7, 1998. I got up at 4 a.m. and read the Morning News and Wall Street Journal. I swam and worked out at the spa from 6 to 7:20. I drove to the Renaissance Hotel for the 8 a.m. Teacher of the Year breakfast. I sat with some teachers and a board member named, John Dodd. John is a nice guy with a wonderful sense of humor. Every one of the approximately 125 teachers present was introduced. On the table were 3x5 index cards. They asked each teacher to write something about their school and share with the table. The activity was fun and interesting. I shared how great the Gooch teachers were and that I admired and loved them. I said that Gooch was the best schoolhouse in Texas! I Left about 10:30 and came home to change my suit and tie. The rest of the day at school went very well.

The next week my principal, Ron Powell, and I attended an ice cream social given for all the Teachers of the Year. It was held in downtown Dallas at the former railroad station. I met Mr. Powell there, and we took a table. I saw my first principal, Ms. Zimny, with whom I had a pleasant, but short conversation. Several people gave speeches and each teacher was introduced. Ron and I were polite and enjoyed some ice cream, but got the hell out of there as fast as we could.

Earlier in the book I related my professional biography and educational history. So here I will share my Philosophy of Teaching, Educational Issues and Trends, my views on the Teaching Profession, and the message for State Teacher of the Year, which I was not selected for by the way.

MY PHILOSOPHY OF TEACHING

As a special education teacher of autistic students I consider these important traits to cultivate:

- I always maintain a positive attitude toward my students. I never give up on them, and I am determined to help them reach their full potential, whatever that may be.

- I realize that patience and understanding seems to help my students make progress and to soothe their sensitive needs.

- My three assistants and I work with a team spirit, which is necessary to coordinate the input we get from many specialists, community agencies, administrators, parents, relatives, and advocates. We see the child in both similar and different aspects that must be made to work in the most positive manner for the student.

- I attempt to maintain a sense of humor. In special education it helps to do this because you constantly deal with the unexpected. I feel my teaching reflects these traits because it's reflected in the climate of the classroom. The students get off the school bus in the morning smiling and are happy to be in class.

- My three assistants and I work harmoniously together and are consistent in application of these traits. We all tremendously enjoy our students.

- I feel the parents have a deep sense of security in regard to their children's placement in our classroom. We maintain daily communication with all parents by personal interaction or by telephone. We make use of each student's daily communication notebook, which goes home each evening.

EDUCATIONAL AND ISSUES AND TRENDS

The following are the major Issues in public education. I will choose one to discuss.

1. Enhance community involvement, which includes financial support, services, human resources, and supplies to insure success for each student.

2. Improve reading literacy for students.

3. Discipline of students and improved safety for students and staff.

4. Successful assimilation of all nationalities, races, and religions so all students have equal opportunity to be successful.

I have chosen Community Involvement, because in my experience community involvement has been most beneficial to my students. Through this involvement I have observed how the individual lives of my students have been improved. Autistic children live in their own little world, which makes being involved in the community even more critical. A large part of our program is to provide outside exposure to enhance social goals, which they seem to be most lacking in. For example, in our class we have benefitted from sports programs and buddy programs with general education students, as well as corporate and community volunteers. Our after school program involves two of our students who get to participate in some regular school programs and activities with community groups. One of most successful is our annual Christmas party with the Disabled American Wheelchair Veterans.

In my opinion, the DPS and community groups have accomplished many great achievements. I admire their progress and salute all who are currently involved and those who have been involved in the past. Given this statement, I will not use the word resolution but will make the following suggestions for continued success:

- Autistic students require more after school programs since most are not accepted in regular programs. This is because more adults are needed to supervise fewer children. I know of one excellent program at a Dallas recreation center but because of limited adult supervision, has only a few autistic students in the program.

- Respite care could be provided for students, which would greatly benefit parents. In most cases regular child-care personnel can't keep autistic children due to their behavior, unusual circumstances, and lack of communication skills. Providing temporary individual care would allow parents a well-deserved break.

- Strengthen support groups. Parents, relatives, and friends of autistic children face some common life situations in regard to the children. There are already some good support groups but I feel community resources could strengthen and expand participation and resulting benefits. For example, an autistic health fair which features facilities, refreshments, fun games, and learning opportunities.

- Awareness programs about autism are needed. This involves speakers, training programs, and public relations. For example, a pro-active awareness program could work with newspapers to print interesting and realistic stories.

The above ideas are very general. I do not claim to be an expert, but I continue to learn more and more every day from my autism students.

THE TEACHING PROFESSION

To strengthen and improve the teaching profession, I believe these factors are necessary:

- It is important to work closely with other school teachers and staff to assure smooth and continuous coordination of class and school activities. This includes unselfish sharing of resources and utilizing the talents of all staff including teachers, administrators, therapists, assistants, cafeteria and custodial personnel.

- We should continue to accept and appreciate corporate and community volunteers. It's good to work with these volunteers in a cordial and open manner and to frequently let them know their good and constructive contributions are very important.

- We should show empathy for parents of autistic students. It's important to work and communicate with parents while understanding that sometimes frustrations and different viewpoints will surface. I believe being positive and viewing the holism of the students' progress is necessary for relations with parents.

- Enrolling in workshops, staff development, and evening courses that are appropriate and beneficial is important. Given the selection of many choices, time and effort should be devoted to the specific selections promising favorable direct and timely results.

- A key to success is participation in mentor and career pro-grams to strengthen the future teaching profession. I like to speak to friends and acquaintances that are interested in being future teachers. I stress the positives of teaching in a realistic manner. I'm truthful in telling them it's a hard job in many ways but that teaching is a very gratifying and worthy profes-sion in all ways.

- Maintain a caring supportive environment for substitute teachers. I'm glad to help and be friendly toward our school substitute teachers because they play a key role in our overall success.

- We should utilize parent, administrative staff, therapist, and volunteer support wisely to assure success. It's vital to pro-cess all advice and facts because good intentions alone, with-out full planning, can lead to detrimental results and negative relationships.

- We should take full advantage of opportunities for positive interactions with other school staff. This includes casual con-versations, school activities, or outside fun activities. For example, my wife and I hosted several baby showers at our home. Since we live near the school it was convenient for everyone to come after school.

STATE TEACHER OF THE YEAR

I would encourage all teachers that we must do the very best job we can as professional educators. We must take care of ourselves physically, mentally, and emotionally. We also must take care of our families.

We must be honest with ourselves and realize that we will have many successes and at times non-successes. We educators must accept and learn from both and move on with our lives as professionals, as individuals, as members of our families, and as members of our community.

There are many elements which contribute to overall achievements:

- Maintain a professional attitude and appearance.

- Be confident enough to be yourself.

- Care for and love students. There is something to love about every student.

- Accept others while listening to and respecting their opinions.

- Do not be afraid to reach out for help when needed and be willing to give help.

- Work within the structure of the school and district guidelines and policies.

Lastly, I'd say specifically to teachers, "Do not lose sight of your important role as a teacher. Challenge always, understand and learn from failures, encourage continually, share in successes, and praise often." Remember our students who are learners today are leaders tomorrow.

As I related earlier I did not win State Teacher of the year, but was not disappointed. I was however surprised that I won Teacher of the Year and was proud that my fellow faculty members felt I deserved the award.

The following is the thank you note I wrote to the staff at Tom Gooch.

> Dear Gooch "Gator" Staff,
>
> I'd sincerely like to thank you for voting me Teacher of the Year. From my viewpoint, let me say this to you my friends, it is my pleasure to simply be a teacher among the many of you truly great teachers. A special thanks to my wonderful assistants who shared in this honor.
>
> You are all very special!
>
> Bob

Another honor, that took me by surprise, was an article included in the DISD newsletter. The article was titled "Reaching the Unreachable."

REACHING THE UNREACHABLE

As a U.S. Air force veteran and oil industry manager, Bob Anterhaus had seen and done it all, traveling and living around the world for 25 years. Of course that all changed when the oil industry went bust in the early 1990's.

Anterhaus was living in Dallas and tutoring at J.P. Starks Elementary School in his free time when his oil industry job was phased out. His wife, Joanne, a retired special education teacher, encouraged Anterhaus to apply for Dallas Public Schools' Alternative Certification Program.

"I was exposed to working with autistic students during my training and found that I was good at it." he said. "It ended up becoming a great experience."

After Anterhaus earned his certification, he was assigned to Walnut Hill Elementary School for three years to teach Total Communication to autistic students. He's been teaching – and learning – the subject at Tom C. Gooch Elementary School for the last four years.

Total Communication focuses on three key primary areas of learning:

- Communication

- Social skills

- independent living and functioning skills

"The program utilizes written and oral words, pictures and objects as tools," he said. "They are used by the autistic students in the classroom as well as outside the school environment."

Anterhaus' job was tough at first, but he followed a simple rule that has always helped him succeed in the past – learn from your surroundings.

"I'm always learning something – from my students and three assistants – every day," he said. "That's the key to my success: learn something new every day and apply it to my job."

Anterhaus is always on the lookout for new teaching methods. For example, he said, the puzzles may spark an interest in the student, and the teacher can work and build on that interest. Another example might be if a student shows interest in blocks. The teacher, then, building on that interest, can have the student match colored blocks or teach him how to count them and sort them out by size.

The seven-year veteran's efforts and effectiveness were rewarded last spring when he was selected Teacher of the Year by his co-workers at Gooch.

Awarded Teacher of the Year by the Tom Gooch faculty for the 1998-1999 school year

"I'm really not the greatest expert in this field," he said. "But if you learn to incorporate all of those great ideas from your co-workers, new teaching methods, plus discover you students' strengths and specific skills, you, too, can reach those students who were once deemed unreachable."

CHAPTER 10
MOVING ON TO BEN MILAM

I WAS STILL AT TOM GOOCH ELEMENTARY SCHOOL at the end of my sixth year of teaching. However, I only had two students left in my class at year's end. The autism director made the decision to send them to another school in order to clear the way for me to be sent to an autism unit at North Dallas High School. At that time, I didn't feel like I was up to teaching in a high school environment, so I indicated as such to the director. I expressed my feelings openly and honestly and told her that I would be considering retirement.

The director did not say anything at the time, but later that day I learned my assistant, Barbara, and I were to be reassigned to a new autism unit being formed at Ben Milam Elementary School. I guess she didn't like the idea of me retiring and did some shifting around to accommodate me. The main thing I had going for me was the fact that after nine years, I had become a very good autism teacher. It didn't hurt that in the DISD there was only a hand full of autism teachers with my tenure. In fact many of the teachers who entered the system were gone within a year or two because autism students can be difficult. However, truth be known, most teachers I knew found other things harder to deal with than students, like the parents. Most parents were great, but there remained a few who were in denial and others who expected a miracle, like some of the parents with younger children.

I respected their right to have those feelings, but often times they would threaten and bully the autism teachers. On some occasions they would initiate legal action in hopes of producing a miracle. Unfortunately, all the legal action does is put the principal and administrators on the warpath with their easiest target being the teacher.

Believe me when I say, the administrators will always go for the easiest target. How would I know? Because I was a member of the Alliance of Dallas Educators Union the whole time I was teaching. Joining and taking part in the union is important for all teachers, but especially for the special education teachers. The dues increased each year and by the time I retired they were $47.45 per month. In a manner of speaking the money was well spent. I called it my protection money and likened it to being caught in a dark alley in the worst part of town with only a small 22 caliber revolver for protection. The small gun might not be enough to protect me, but it was better than having nothing.

The Alliance didn't have a lot of power because of the laws in Texas, but over the years, did its best to help the membership. They were usually successful because the DISD gods of war, excuse the expression, found it easier to gather their harvest from the nonunion people that had no protective covering.

One sad incident resulting in detrimental consequences happened to one of my special education teacher friends. Susan

Basement classroom at Ben Milam

thought she didn't need the union because she was in a good school. She was teaching a special education Early Childhood Class for students three to six years old. One of the children had a parent who didn't work and lived near the school. The parent attended every day and even went on field trips with the class. The parent issued some complaint to the principle against Susan and she was placed on paid leave. After a few months, Susan learned she was being sent to another school and into a different program. Susan was an excellent and experienced teacher, but she had no voice or control over what happened.

As you can see by Susan's example a special education teacher who is not a member of the Alliance union is at risk when dealing with a disgruntled parent. Understandably, principals have many issues to consider in the daily running of a school. So often the principals find it is easier to side with the parent, let them know how sorry he or she is, and then toss the qualified teacher into the wind. I have also seen some principals try to appease the parent in an attempt to help the teacher deal with the situation. However, in Susan's case, not having union representation, the situation led her down a dead end street.

Another serious challenge facing teachers is all the paperwork and reports required. Many of the reports are the result of our assiduous Uncle Sam's involvement in our schools. Most families have an aunt, uncle, cousin, grandparent, or other relative who is wonderfully unique. Those families learn to accept the relative for who they are. Uncle Sam, our country loves you even though you take a nip or two out of our derrieres now and then. I sincerely mean what I say, because I have visited many countries and wouldn't trade our Uncle Sam. I'm overjoyed every time I return to the USA from any other country. Uncle Sam, I will propose a toast, "To better times ahead because the best is yet to come."

FIRST YEAR AT MILAM

The new class at Milam was formed from students who had been moved from different schools. We had five of the hardest students, two students with unhappy parents and my two assistants. You might say it was the director's way of getting even with me for not going to North Dallas High School. But hey, all is fair in love and war and I was overjoyed to be at Ben Milam.

Barbara, whom I had requested to be moved with me, was also happy. When I started writing the book, she was still employed and I am sure happy being at Milam. I haven't returned to the school since my retirement, because I miss the school and kids. It just still hurts too much for me to return. Joanne and I were invited to the annual winter break dinner, which was held at a Mexican restaurant on December 15, 2011. It was the first time since retiring that I had seen and spoken to Barbara. I received a service recognition award and the inscription read, "In appreciation for 20 years of outstanding teaching and service to the children and community of the Dallas Independent School District." The award meant a lot to me, and to this day I have it hanging in my office. It was the best gift Ms. Gamez, the Ben Milam Principal, and the school staff could have given me.

That first year at Milam was by far the hardest year I had endured in my career. One boy, who's cognitive level was less than one year, could run as fast as a deer, and would sometimes run away while tipping over furniture. Another autistic boy, Alex, was smart in many ways, but very violent at times. The principal at the time, Ms. Brackenridge, suggested I needed a third assistant. I told her I did not want a third, because previously I had three assistants and they developed problems among themselves. Fortunately Ms. Brackenridge overruled me, and hired Karin.

Karin was a nice lady from Honduras where she had also been a teacher. She worked during the day, as an assistant, with me at Ben Milam and attended evening classes at the University of Texas at Arlington. She was studying to become a regular education teacher. Soon after Karin started she was walking Alex to the after school bus and he started punching her. He was almost as tall and outweighed her. The altercation caused her to cry, but single handed she kept her composure, gained control of him and got him safely on the bus. Karin was not only smart, but a tough gal. She was one of the best assistants I ever had, and we became good friends.

Having three good assistants helped me in many ways. They were obviously a big help with the students. However, it was not uncommon for me to spend several hours a day filling out reports and completing the necessary documentation the school required. Because of their presence, oftentimes I was freed up to work at my desk. Another benefit was that if an assistant was out sick or took a personal day, we could more easily continue the normal class day while still assuring student safety.

SCHOOL RATING

I paid my dues, especially during the first two years at Milam, teaching autism. I knew a lot about autism but not much about general education. Every year the school kids took state tests and once the results were in for the current year our school was rated as "low performing."

Our new status resulted in visits from a lot of "nice people" throughout the school year. These people were mostly concerned with the regular education teachers, but they were required to visit and interview every teacher. Jeremy, a teacher friend of mine, filled me in on the questions they would be asking and the proper answers to give. Sure enough, when I was interviewed, they asked the same questions so I was prepared.

As it turned out, our principal had allowed students from across town to attend our school. Due to test results from those few students we were just barely put in the low performing category. At the time, I remember being proud of our Principal and our excellent school. However, I was also concerned about the wasteful spending that resulted from our low standing. Finishing up one of the interviews, I asked the man interviewing where he was from and he told me he was a principal out in West Texas. Later I thought, "He sure is a long way from his school district." Someone is paying for his hotels, meals, airfare or mileage, and other costs. The interview raised two simple questions for me. Could it be that our good ole Uncle Sam shelled out the loot? Didn't we have people living in Dallas who could help remedy our dire need to get off the hit list and assure our salvation? Sure would have saved money by eliminating travel costs.

After one year, we were again an acceptable rated school. Adios to our pals! *Gracias, pero que esperamos y oramos que nunca necesitamos su ayuda de nuevo* (thanks, but we hope and pray we never need your help again.)

BEN MILAM PRINCIPALS

During my tenure at Ben Milam I was fortunate to have three excellent principals. They were excellent at their job, caring and easy to talk to. The staff, students, and parents were blessed to have them. They were a big advantage for all of us, because depending on the effectiveness of the principal, there is a distinct determination whether a school is good or bad. The reverse is true; a bad principal can drag a school downhill fast. I am happy to state that in all my years of teaching there was only one principal that I considered bad. Thus, I knew from personal experience what a good or bad principle could mean for a school.

My first principal was Ms. Brackenridge. Joanne and I first met her a few weeks before school started. The only people present were Ms. Brackenridge and her secretary. After talking with her, looking around, and getting the feel of the school, we knew everything was going to be all right. During her tenure at the school everyone I knew greatly liked and respected Ms. Brackenridge.

Unfortunately, about the time we received a rating as a low performing school, we were informed she had developed a medical situation that caused her to leave school. She was later transferred to administration within the DISD. We all missed her. I've run into and spoken to her at a few functions over the years and it is always a pleasure.

Ms. Vail took Ms. Brackenridge's place arriving a month or two after the school year had started. Since we were rated as a low performing school, she was going to get a lot of "friendly help" from the local and state people. I honestly thought administration was going to send us a "Gestapo" type of new principal. My friend Jeremy told me he had seen the new principal and that she had blond hair. Later in the day, I saw Ms. Vail at a distance on the playground and immediately thought, "This lady doesn't look like Gestapo." My fears were groundless because she was a good principal in all respects. During her tenure our school received a positive rating and was no longer considered low performing.

We all knew because of her young age she would eventually be leaving us. Frequently, she would be called out of school to attend various training classes. Prior to assuming the head principal role at Ben Milam she had been an assistant principal at Woodrow High School. Ms. Vail and her father had both graduated from Woodrow Wilson so she longed to return. Sure enough, after a few years at Ben Milam she was promoted to be the head principal at Woodrow. We hated to lose her, but were happy, Woodrow Wilson was lucky to get her back. We all knew she would be an excellent high school principal, and we were thankful for the time we had her at Ben Milam.

My last principal was Ms. Gamez and the one I had the longest. She was very hard working and a leader of the other principals in our area quadrant. Each year, I feared the powers to be would scoop her up and promote her into an administrative position. We loved her and enjoyed our success under her tenure.

I learned a great deal from these principals and the regular teachers. Ben Milam really had an exceptional staff. It was a small school, and many of the teachers were veterans with many years' experience. We worked together closely and they were glad to meet with me, give me advice, or to share their ideas about how we could help the students. I learned a lot about teaching by being in their classrooms, watching them teach their daily lessons, and being part of their class learning process. At the end of each year, I wrote thank you cards to each of the teachers I had worked with. I thanked them for all they had taught the students and especially for all they taught me. It is my belief that they knew I sincerely appreciated working with them and I meant what I said.

CHAPTER 11
TRANSITION INTO RESOURCE AND INCLUSION AT BEN MILAM

AFTER ELEVEN YEARS, I was considered an expert in autism, but knew little else. My friend Jeremy taught resource and inclusion, which is special education, but working with general education students in the special education classroom or in the students' regular classrooms. These students mostly need help in reading. However, occasionally they needed help in other subjects. Jeremy told me his overall goal was to move from teaching into administration. I shared with my wife Joanne what he said, and she quickly suggested I should change jobs with him.

Her suggestion made absolutely no sense to me, but after we talked through the situation I understood and agreed with her reasoning. Many of the disabled were being diagnosed as autistic, which meant that a lot of funding and resources were being spent on autism. Many famous sports people, actors, actresses, and other well-known stars had autistic children of their own and were active in addressing a cure. An administrator without autism teaching experience is like a second lieutenant leading troops into combat. The troops want to follow someone who has combat experience not someone who just came out of the military academy.

I explained the reasoning to Jeremy and he agreed it was a logical move for him. He struggled with the decision, because he knew better than anyone how difficult my class was and the lack of assistance he and I could expect from the administration at the DISD. I told Jeremy, as well as several others, that he was one of the bravest men I ever met and we needed him on the front line. We spoke to our principal, Ms. Vail toward the end of the school year and she agreed to make the swap at the start of the next new school year.

Jeremy was nervous about the move, but he was not the only one, I had very little experience working with regular students. Truthfully, I was concerned whether I could excel in the area. For eleven years my experience had been teaching severely disabled autistic students. I had been teaching functional skills, such as using utensils for eating, going to the bathroom, or doing assigned work tasks. I taught social skills, such as sitting still when appropriate, not taking others' food or toys, and waiting in line. However, in resource and inclusion classes, I was going to be teaching, reading, math, and science to regular education students with learning difficulties.

Fortunately, the District had just bought the Saxon Reading Program, an extensive and scripted program with over one hundred thirty lessons. I spent hours studying the program along with other reading, language arts, and math learning programs. I also worked closely with the regular teachers to get both work and advice from them. They were all very cooperative and a great ben-efit to both me and the students.

The last school year, I started at Milam with no class, so I worked with non-special education students in need of extra help. I found my efforts very rewarding and not much different from working with the special education students. I learned something every day from my time working with the students. I also learned more and more about teaching regular education from the teach-ers because of my involvement in their classrooms.

To my delight I excelled with each interaction. I also found that teaching a variety of subjects helped me hone their reading skills. For example, there might be a scientific word they had never seen before, so I was able to show them how to sound out the word phonically to pronounce it correctly. These times were especially effective to instruct the students about words having vowel com-binations.

My first year was the most difficult and I made it through mostly by trial and error. I was assigned a second grader, two fifth graders, and four sixth graders. I worked closely with their regular teachers and often turned to my wife for advice. For the most part I did a good job, but there was one exception.

Pablo was a sixth grader who was mischievous and inert. If you knew him you might assume he was lazy. However, he needed someone with more patience and one-on-one help than I knew how to give him. I think he was the only student in my teaching career that I did not have a good rapport with. Looking back, I feel it was more my fault than Pablo's. I learned patience and persever-ance from Pablo, he taught me a lot. I still think about him from time to time. He is a young adult now and I hope he is doing well and having a good life. If Pablo should read this book, I would like to tell him, "Thanks, Pablo, for making me a better teacher." Pablo is not his real name, but I think if he reads the book he will know it's him I'm thanking.

I had made my share of mistakes, but by the second year I was much better and by the third year I was on a roll. I grew into and became an excellent resource and inclusion teacher.

Many of my students, who tested as special education, were like the regular education students except that they needed extra academic help. A few even performed better than the regular education kids in their class. As a result, some students who were referred for special education did not qualify when tested. Supposedly the test revealed through various labeling reasons that the students were performing at an acceptable academic level and special education would not help them advance. I didn't fully understand why, but attributed the fact to the federal guidelines.

Therefore the government would not provide the necessary funding. Unfortunately, if the school district did not get the funding, the children in need couldn't enter the special education resource and inclusion program. I'm sorry to wake you up, Uncle Sam, but I have a question. Why at times does it take so long to qualify?

I had one student who was tested in third, fourth, and fifth grade, but did not qualify. However, she tested in sixth and did qualify. Since the testing was a long process she was not able to enter the program until the second semester of her sixth grade year. She always tried to do her best, and her parents worked with her at home. Upon completion of our program I continued to see her mother because she had a younger sister enrolled at Ben Milam. I am pleased to say she went on to do very well in middle school where she remained in special education.

I've seen the prolonged process have an adverse effect on many parents and students. Parents felt the district had let them down and would leave upset and often in tears. The regular teachers experience the effects as well, especially since they are the ones who must do a lot of the intervention and documentation before a student can even be tested. They were left feeling like their time would have been better spent in the classroom.

In addition to submitting the child for the program the regular teachers took time out to attend the student support team meetings (SST), which were normally held after school. The SST meeting consisted of the principal, counselor, nurse, three or four teachers, the student's teacher, and parents. All involved were willing to go through the motions knowing we had an excellent program. They knew other students who had made substantial progress in the special education classes. However, once the evaluation was complete they were not pleased to hear, "Sorry the student doesn't qualify, try again next year."

As I have already mentioned teachers are required to do a lot of reports. Many of which were a seemingly a waste of time not serving a constructive purpose. However, there were some reports that were actually beneficial and useful. One in particular was a yearly report and was meaningful for both the principal and the teacher. In the second semester, teachers were required to complete and turn in a professional development and support form prior to their annual evaluation. The form was a teacher self-report; effective tool in helping the teacher consider all they had been doing throughout the year. They were encouraged to reflect back on the positive things they had accomplished while making plans for the future. The information also made their formal evaluation more fair and equitable.

Section I of the report was in a checked format that evaluated contributions to the improvement of academic performance of all students on campus. The following is an excerpt of my report for the 2004-2005 school year when I was teaching resource and inclusion at Ben Milam.

Section II, questions 3 through 9 and my corresponding answers.

3. **Describe a specific instructional adjustment (e.g., materials, sequencing, etc.) which you have made based on the needs assessment of your students.**

In addition to our everyday work in reading for my fifth grade students, I have made structural adjustments using current newspapers, Nation Geographic magazines, Newsweek, etc. I use appropriate articles that are of interest to the students and have learning value.

4. **Describe the approaches you have used to monitor classroom performance and to provide feedback to students regarding their progress in academic skills (TEKS/TAKS objectives).**

I use worksheets and teacher made tests. As an LRE (Least Restrictive Environment) teacher, I consult with the general education teachers about their progress with regular class work. Our work is based on the TAKS objectives, which are incorporated in each special education student's individual objectives, so the students are always up to date on their progress in academic skills.

5. **Describe how you assisted your students who were experiencing serious attendance problems.**

Only one student had attendance problems. I spoke to the general education teacher, and we got the counselor and social worker involved to work with the parent.

6. **Describe your approach in working with students who were failing or in danger of failing.**

The classroom teacher and I incorporate modifications. We design specific work, projects, and learning techniques to help the student.

Our ARD meetings for special education students address the danger of failing and new or revised individual education procedures are made.

7. **List or describe your professional development activities for the past year related to campus/district goals, assigned subject/content, needs of students, or prior appraisal performances in the following areas: in service, team planning, mentoring, collaboration with colleagues, self-study, video coursework or distance learning, university-level coursework, professional conferences, and other non-traditional activities.**

I have taken formal training courses through the DISD, such as Saxon Reading, Inclusion, and Spanish. I have informally learned on my own to increase technology skills and to develop improved teaching methods. I have tutored students in math and reading in the after school program. I frequently consult with the third, fifth, and sixth grade teachers.

8. **As a result of your professional development activities described above, what have you been able to use in your classroom that has positively impacted the learning of students?**

The Saxon Reading Program was new last year, so additional training has allowed me to better understand and teach reading to my students. I was new in LRE last year, so by closely consulting and working with my students' general education teachers I have become a better teacher to impact the learning of my students and regular education students I also work with.

9. Be prepared to discuss three areas for continued professional growth.

My target areas are to continue to advance the Saxon Reading Program, continue to learn conversational Spanish through the DISD program for teachers, and increase my ability to use computer and related technology.

※ ※ ※

I kept my answers fairly short because there was not a lot of space on the form, and I wanted to answer in a manner that was short and direct. I was happy to help with the evaluation process in any way I could, because the work load placed on principals continues to increase and become more complicated.

For example, at many of the workshops teachers were required to attend, principals were the class instructors instead of administrators. Personally, I believe it was one of the smartest decisions made in the DISD. I told my principal at Ben Milam, Ms. Gamez, that I was glad principals, rather than administrators, were teaching workshops because they live in the "real world" of education while many of the administrators do not. The experience would also help them to better relate to teachers and students. She said she would pass it along to her area supervisor. I don't know if she ever did, but by saying she would pass it on, made me feel good.

I continued teaching in the area for the next eight years at Ben Milam. My students were in the first to sixth grades. Later it was only to fifth grade because sixth grade was moved to middle school. Each year, I would have students in two, three, or four different grades. For the resource students, I would pull them from class and take them to my classroom where I would teach reading, math, or both. Most students usually only required reading assistance. For the inclusion students, I would visit them in their regular classroom and work with them alone or in a small group setting along with some of the regular education students. Sometimes we would work at a table in the hall. The teachers would normally provide me with their assigned work, which I would follow. At other times, I brought my own work for the students.

When asked, I gladly attended field trips with the classes, especially when I knew I could be of help. Some teachers wanted me to go so I could help with and monitor the special education students. Other teachers didn't think to ask. Of course, it didn't bother me because I had numerous students in other grades to take care of who were not going on field trips. What an amazing job I had, and I got paid for doing it!

CHAPTER 12
WHAT I LEARNED ABOUT AUTISM

BEFORE BEGINNING my career teaching autistic students, I probably knew more about the subject of autism than the average person. My stepson Warren is disabled, so over the years, I have met and interacted with many disabled individuals and their families.

One of Warren's friends, Gary, is about five years older and has autism on a higher level. Warren and I were privileged to visit Gary at his home and to meet his parents. They had a loving home and Gary was their youngest child and obviously in need of a lot of attention. Gary's parents' main concern was who would take care of him when they reached old age or became ill. I had the honor of taking Warren and Gary fishing on occasion and was able to get to know Gary.

When I was going through the Alternative Education Program I visited several classrooms at the E. D. Walker Special Education

Center. To my surprise Gary was in one of the classes, so I went up and shook hands with him. Not realizing that I knew Gary, one of the assistants warned me to be careful because at times Gary got violent. Standing at 5 foot 6 inches tall I had always found him to be calm. Later, I related my experience to his parents and they told me Gary had developed another side. I soon realized autistic students share some of the same characteristics, but can be different in many ways.

I knew teaching autistic children would present a difficult challenge, but at the same time I was fascinated. I felt it was exactly the right place for me to be. Looking back, I see how the kids truly helped me to have a fuller and happier life. I am also proud to say that my colleagues and I were able to help a plethora of autistic students, their parents, and families. Teaching autistic students was a true blessing in my life. I will always be thankful to my students and their families for that privilege.

CONTINUING EDUCATION

Over the eleven years I taught autism, I became more and more knowledgeable. The best way to learn was by working with the students, assistants, other teachers, parents, and therapists. Sure, I made my share of mistakes, but I attempted to learn from each of those mistakes.

I attended many state and local autism conferences and DISD workshops. For several years, the autism department would invite Dr. Gary Mesibov from the University of North Carolina at Chapel Hill. Twice a year Dr. Mesibov would travel to Dallas to meet with all the autism teachers. UNC has one of the best autism programs in the country. Their autism teaching method is called TEACCH (Treatment and Education of Autistic and Related Communication-Handicapped Children) and is used in the DISD. The method was developed by psychologist Eric Schopler at the University of North Carolina in the 1960's.

At that time, the DISD autism program had an excellent program and reputation. Many families moved to Dallas so that their autistic child could attend the program. Over the years, I had two students whose families moved. One came from Ohio and one from Idaho. There was another family who moved from Hawaii to Dallas to enroll their son in the autism program, but I did not know them.

A TEACCH classroom uses structured teaching with separate defined areas for each task, such as individual work, group activities, and play. The program relies on visual learning. The students use schedules made up of pictures and words to order their day and to help them move smoothly between activities or to answer questions or to make requests.

I attended other conferences at E. D. Walker, two of which had a profound effect on me. Both featured famous early advocates who made the general public fully aware of the characteristics of autism and how it affects them and their families.

The first was Ms. Temple Grandin who herself had a form of high functioning autism. She has her doctorate degree in animal science and consults with the livestock industry on animal behavior. She is also a bestselling author noted for her work in autism advocacy. She spoke about her invention, the squeeze machine, a form of stress relief therapy that she designed at age eighteen. Latter, the machine was used to calm other hypersensitive people. The piece of equipment caught my attention because we had a student in need of this type of therapy. Her name was Stephanie and the program called for us to wrap her from the shoulders down to her waist with a sort of rubber elastic that was four inches in width. We had to put her arms straight down so she could be wrapped. Stephanie knew where the wrap was kept and she would nod her head to show that she wanted to be wrapped.

At various times through the years, before paperwork and administrators took charge of the funds, the DISD Autism program included swimming, ice skating, a trip to the annual Texas State Fair, and bowling. We didn't have the funding to do all the activities so we rotated the activities on an annual basis. One time we had taken the class to a bowling alley and Stephanie suddenly wanted to be wrapped. We quickly wrapped her not sensing the attention we were creating and the hard stares from many people in the bowling alley. I didn't notice the stares, because I was too busy helping the students and keeping them from dropping the balls on their feet. Later, I learned from a therapist with us, that we had gained the attention of many people in the bowling alley. We felt this was okay, because dealing with autism you just keep trucking along and do what works for the success of each student.

The second was Dr. Bernard Rimland who was an American research psychologist, writer, lecturer, and advocate for children with autism, ADHD, learning disabilities, and mental retardation. Dr. Rimland was based in San Diego, California. In 1965 he founded the Autism Society of America and in 1967 he founded the Autism Research Institute. He was the father of a high-functioning autistic son.

Dr. Rimland was the primary technical advisor on autism for the 1988 move "Rain Man," which helped establish awareness of autism. The main character in the movie, played by Dustin Hoffman, had what is called savant syndrome. A person with savant syndrome has a serious mental and or autistic disorder, but with an incredible talent. They often border on genius. I found the movie to be of great interest, but out of the hundreds of autistic students I observed over the years, I only observed one savant similar to the character in the movie.

Chou was a nine year old dinosaur savant, which meant he was expert about dinosaurs. He absolutely loved them and could name all of them and spell their names too. At times when I would misspell a name, he would quickly stop and correct me. When I moved to the inclusion area, his new teacher, who knew a lot about technology, got him interested in using the computer. After one year Chou's parents moved to another city. We were sorry to see him leave.

MR. BOB AND HIS STUDENTS

The students had a hard time with my last name, so instead of calling me Mr. Anterhaus I had them call me Mr. Bob. It would be difficult to share all my experiences; however I would like to share a few that still hold special meaning for me.

- **James** who was one of the first students to attend my 3 to 5 year old class. I had him for several years because I was transferred to the older class after two years. James could not speak, but was a very smart boy. Three memories come to mind about James:

  My assistant was at lunch and I was alone with the students. I turned on soft music, lowered the lights down, and had them nap on mats under their desks. During this time I would write in their daily notebooks that went home to their parents. I looked up and saw James rolling a ball toward me. I rolled it back and he flipped it in his hands and rolled it back to me. I attempted the same motion and sent it back to him. He did another unusual motion, and I did the same. About the time James laid back down a physical therapist walked in and saw only me sitting by my desk laughing holding a ball in my hand.

I thought, "Oh well, in special education it helps to have a sense of humor."

Another memory about James was the time some ladies came into our room wearing full skirts. James ran under their skirts, needless to say, they were somewhat surprised.

The last memory of James I want to share involved a tragic event. The bus driver told us that James' apartment burned down. Fortunately, no one had been hurt. His brother blamed James for the fire. Knowing James and some things that happened previously with his brother, I think that his brother who was playing with matches caused the fire and blamed it on James. I didn't know for sure, so I kept the thought to myself. We took up a collection at school and sent money and clothes to the family.

- **Juan** was a well behaved boy. He could not speak, but seemed to enjoy the work jobs we gave him. He liked to draw pictures on his own. He was the only autistic student I ever saw who could draw in three dimension. For example, he drew buildings in the correct perspective with the corners and sides true to scale.

  I had Juan for only one year. Juan had a young mother from Central America and an older father I had never met. Unfortunately, his parents broke up and his mother moved him to another school district. If students stayed in the DISD I could keep track of them by talking to their teachers at meetings and could see how they and their parents were doing. Sadly, if they left the district like Juan, I couldn't find out how they were doing. This caused me to lose track of many of my students over the years.

- **Toby** was one of the students I had in both my first school and second schools. His favorite thing to do was to take a piece of string and continuously twirl it in his hand. He hated to do his assigned work tasks. I was firm with him, but tried to assign jobs he might be more interested in. I would make up jobs using items I purchased from garage sales or ideas I got from reading magazines.

  Initially, if I didn't stay right by Toby, he would quit working. However, as a result of trying the different one-on-one job tasks he started doing the work on his own. One of the autism administrators who knew Toby came to my class and saw Toby working by himself at his desk. She looked at me with astonishment and exclaimed, "That boy is actually working." Toby's parents were from Africa and had three other regular education children. For some reason they decided to send Toby back to Africa to live on a farm with his grandmother. I lost touch with him until several years later.

  One of our DISD diagnosticians let me know that Toby had returned from Africa and she had tested him at one of the DISD high schools. She told me that he was not doing his work and got violent when prompted to do so. Toby's mother had shown her a picture that was taken with Toby and me at Tom Gooch when he received an award. His mother related how proud she had been of the progress he had been making. She related to her that she had no choice other than to send him back to live with his grandmother at the time. The diagnostician thought I would like to know.

- **Arlene** was one of the few girls I had in the nine years at my first two schools. Before the assessment of autism was greatly expanded, most of the autism students were male. When

Arlene's parents divorced, her mother moved back to Dallas from another state. Her brother who was in regular education stayed with the father. The only words Arlene could say were, "Oh No!" I think she had heard her mom say these words on many occasions. The two of them weighed the same and with her mother's medical issues it was difficult for her to handle Arlene.

It was suggested by one of the therapist that I should get a one-on-one assistant for Arlene because she ran around the room, tipped over furniture, and would not listen to directions. I went along with the idea and asked for an assistant. One of the special education administrators came out and seemed to be in agreement. Before leaving, he gave me the forms, which would be necessary to justify the need for an assistant. I started filling them out, but after a few days I thought it would be better if my assistant and I just rotated working one-on-one with Arlene. In autism, we used many tools to establish and maintain two-way communication. We were thrilled when they succeeded. When Arlene ran, we made her sit right next to one of us. When she tipped furniture, with our assistance, we required her to pick the item up and put it back where it belonged. When she completed the work jobs, we rewarded her success. We utilized several different rewards and varied them for daily activities.

One reward she liked was to sit on our small trampoline after she finished her work job. Before the semester ended we came to understand each other. For example, she went to tip over a chair over, but first put her hands on the chair and looked at me. I stood with my arms on my hips and gave her a stern look. She looked at me for a few seconds, then smiled, and walked away from the chair. I will never forget that smile, I think

Arlene got the last laugh on me, but that's okay because she left a fond memory that I treasure. When Arlene's mother died she left DISD to live with her father. Unfortunately, I was out of school the day her father took her, so I did not get to say goodbye.

- **Kevin** was a good student who did his job tasks and exercised good behavior. He did one unusual thing that I had never seen any other student do. Whenever Kevin saw a pile of dog manure, he would run to it and stomp on it with both feet. We would watch Kevin closely when we took walks in the neighborhood. Walks outside of the school have not been allowed now for a number of years, but they were very good for our students. The walks helped them to relax and to learn the importance of safety, verbal communication, and social skills with the group. One year we participated in a swimming program and took the kids by bus to a local DISD pool once a week for six weeks. On one occasion, upon exiting the bus, Kevin spotted a large dog pile, and before anyone could stop him he was stomping away. I had my assistants take the students inside while I sat on the curb cleaning Kevin's shoes with sticks and leaves. It was just another day in the life of an autism teacher's life. We learned to go with the flow and rarely had a problem because we were multi-talented.

- **Al** who was in fourth grade could speak fairly well, was cooperative, and liked to do his work jobs. I took him to some of the regular classes and stayed with him. Three memories come to mind about Al. I had taken him to a regular music class and when the teacher asked a question, Al would quickly raise his hand. When the teacher called on Al, he would answer in what appeared to be a foreign language. At the time, I thought it sounded like Chinese. Afterwards, I shared the event with his mother and she told me Al spoke only English. She had never heard him speak in the way I described. All the kids liked Al, so we let him respond before moving on to the next question.

The second memory was the time I took him to library. The teacher had the kids sit on the floor as she read a story and I took a seat behind Al. I had worked out at the spa that morning and was feeling pretty relaxed listening to the teachers soothing voice. In fact, so much so, I dozed off. When the story was over, Al tapped on my shoe waking me, and we left to return to our room.

The third memory occurred as I was putting students on the bus after school. Al's mother always came to pick him up after the busses were loaded. So I would take him with me to see the kids off and then we would return to our room. One day, as I was loading the students, Al started walking away toward the front of the school and wouldn't listen to my calls for him to return. I began following and quickened my step in an attempt to catch up with him. However, this caused him to walk faster. So I stopped and to my surprise he stopped. I continued the chase and he stayed about ten paces ahead of me. We walked around to the other side of the school. There were quite a few parents on each side of the school at the time that got a kick out of watching the two of us. Finally, tired of playing the game I ran and caught up with him and escorted him back to the classroom. I took him by the hand back to the classroom.

I had several students who were what we called "runners," and I knew to watch them closely. Al only ran once, so we didn't feel he fit in the same category. My recollection at the time was that he was playing a game. He was one of the many students who helped me to develop a sixth sense while working with my autistic students.

- **Cassey** was in my class for one year before moving on to middle school. He was well behaved, mostly quiet, could understand what we said, and did as we asked. A few years later, I met his middle school teacher at a workshop and asked about him. She told me Cassey had died during a seizure, which was his first. He always appeared to be healthy, so I was shocked and very sorry about his death.

- **Larry** walked slowly and with a slight limp. We did not categorize him as a runner, but he would wait for just the right time and then do a disappearing act. I lost him two times.

  The first time was during our class at Walnut Hill. There was a lot of activity in the room and I was alone with the students. Larry opened the door, sneaked out, and quietly closed the door behind him. He started walking the long hallway toward the door leading outside when a teacher spotted him and brought him back to our class. Unfortunately, she went to the principal's office and squealed.

  However, I knew that many of the principals used teachers and especially assistants as their moles (tattle tales) so I decided to go straight to the principal's office. I thought it wise that she hear about the incident directly from me. She met me in the hallway and I related the experience and offered a solution. I suggested we install a wooden baby gate at the door. The idea worked well because the students could not undo the latch.

  The second time we lost Larry was on a field trip to the Dallas Zoo. We had been walking around for quite some time and decided to stop at the bathroom. We had two autism classes and several parents with us, including Larry's mother. When we came out and counted heads Larry was gone. Not finding him in the bathroom, we left a teacher, assistant, and a few parents with the kids and the rest of us headed in different directions. Fortunately, we found him unharmed. When we returned to school, I told his mother how sorry I was. She then related a story about when they lived in Tennessee near a wooded area.

She was taking Larry's younger brother out of his car seat when she looked up and saw Larry nowhere in sight. In a state of panic, she asked for help and the locals assembled a search party to look for him. When they found Larry in the woods, he was excited and wanted to continue thinking it was a game. No one seemed to share his excitement. I can tell you, the two times I lost Larry, I was pretty excited, but not in a good way. Those were not fun times for me.

- **Alex** would say some words, but couldn't speak in sentences. However, he was a smart boy and especially liked for me to work with him on his daily job tasks. His mother worked on the weekends so his older brother would watch him in her absence. For no apparent reason, Alex started urinating in a cup or on the floor in our classroom. We were confused because he was fully potty trained. Of course, we quickly got him to stop by taking him to the bathroom several times during the day. We suspected, but could not prove that Alex's brother had been locking him up in a closet and forcing him to use a cup or the floor when he had to go.

   Sadly, we had to watch him closely because he could be violent at times, especially with classmates. So on nice days, to help ease his tension, I would take him out to the playground with the rest of the class. However, on cold days or days when it was slightly raining I would take Alex out alone and leave my assistants with the students. Alex loved playing on the playground and climbing on the equipment. I could have gotten in trouble for taking him out alone. There were rules about not going outside when the temperature was below a certain level or if it was an ozone day. I made it a point to follow the multitude of rules, regulations, and calamitous canons, although at times they had to be slightly bent in order to benefit my students. In Alex's case I was happy to bend the rules.

- I knew **Sara** because she had been in my wife's class in another school. However, after being diagnosed as autistic, she was enrolled in my class at Ben Milam. Sara was a good student, had good social skills and was able, with a little help, to complete her work tasks. After her parents divorced, we were told she started having difficulties at home where she lived with her mother and brother. My assistants and I will never forget one award assembly where Sara startled us all.

Every six weeks the school held an award assembly. Our class consisted of seven students and we always attended the morning assembly with the lower grades. The higher grade levels had their award ceremony in the afternoon. We gave awards for the most social skills, best class friend, most improved, best class helper, for class projects, or whatever we thought they deserved for that six weeks. We would give our awards out first and then leave since there were so many children in attendance. The ceremony had gone exceptionally well, but as we started to leave the stage, Sara yelled out clearly, "F*** Y**!" There was total silence from the numerous parents, including Sara's mother, who were in attendance. Of course, my assistants and I just acted as if nothing had happened and escorted the students out.

A TYPICAL DAY IN AN AUTISM CLASSROOM

The structure of each autism class is similar in most respects, but differs depending on the age of the students, functional capacity of the students, and how many assistants are assigned to the teacher. This was especially the case when we went on field trips, attended school events, had visits from therapists, teachers, assistants or others from outside the school. The following will give you an idea of a normal day in a third to sixth grade autism class.

7:45 to 8:15: Parents or busses bring the students to school. Upon arrival the children choose a favorite book or a quiet activity to do.

8:15 to 8:20: Listen to the Pledge of Allegiance and school announcements.

8:20 to 9:00: Breakfast in the cafeteria and then take the students for a rest room break.

9:00 to 9:45 – Individual work time. Sitting at his or her own desk area each student works on five different job tasks. Jobs are individually chosen for each student. The teacher and assistants move from student to student to observe or help the student.

9:45 to 10:15: Outdoor activities. If the weather is bad, activities are done in the classroom using special equipment such as foam balls, hand objects to squeeze, expandable tunnel for the kids to crawl through, and a small trampoline.

10:15 to 10:30: Hygiene time. Kids wash their hands and use restroom. We change diapers at this time and throughout the day as necessary. One or more students could be wearing a diaper.

10:30 to 11:00: Circle time and leisure time. Based on the weekly lesson plan the teacher reads a book, explains the wording, and then asks students about the color pictures.

11:00 to 11:30: Lunch in the cafeteria. Some students will bring a lunch from home, but most will eat in the cafeteria. We use the microwave in the room to heat lunches brought from home before heading to the cafeteria.

11:30 to 12:00 – Return to room. Brush teeth and use restroom.

12:00 to 1:00: Relaxing time. Soft music is played and students draw or work on puzzles, crafts, or other favorite activity.

1:00 to 2:00: Introduction of new job tasks. Work on class project. For example, preparing a hallway bulletin board.

2:00 to 2:30: Snack time and clean up.

2:30 to 3:00: Preparation to leave. Pack bags, use the bathroom, change diapers, and write notes to the parents in the student notebooks sent home each afternoon.

At various times throughout the day we would also incorporate activities which kept the student's interest and avoided down time. These activities could be used for individual students or as a group activity. Let's look at four major strategy areas:

1. Sensory Exploration Time

We organized activities using sand tubs, water or bean trays, foam soap or shaving cream, toys or implements that buzzed, shook, or had a fuzzy feeling. The types of items used during this time were deemed cause and effect. I personally had a lot of students who preferred our rocking chairs and trampolines. An Occupational Therapist would come one day a week during this time and bring her own items to work with the students. Items like: goo, balls, toys or puppets like Elmo. My assistants and I would help her and observe what worked so we could incorporate the same or similar activity into our daily routine.

2. Music

Most all of the students liked music. We listened to music for group enjoyment and during our relaxing time from noon to one o clock. Occasionally we used headphones, but mostly we utilized music to involve the students. We had them dance with each other, but this wouldn't last long, so one of the staff would dance with each student while playing the music they liked. A more complex activity involved turning the music on and off. They would be working alone or in a group and if the music stopped they were to stop. When the music started they were to start. We also had a music therapist visit one day a week for an hour. She brought a guitar and other simple music instruments that she would play. She also let the students play and they enjoyed the time immensely.

3. Social Time

Autistic children tend to ignore other students and show little interest in regular social activities. Throughout the day, we used various activities to encourage the students to interact with each other. We also had students interact with any adults visiting the class. This was especially the case during circle time, out on the playground, and when therapists came to work with our students. The only exception was during individual work time or meal times.

4. Language Activities

We used picture and word communication cards for students to communicate. In the DISD, we used the Boardmaker System. In most cases, students used the same cards, but there were times we used cards made specifically for each student. Many students found the cards advantageous to communicate and fulfill their wants and needs.

We also used computer programs and other devices to increase language skills. We had students who never uttered a word, some who used a few words or short sentences, and others who had fairly good vocabularies. When possible we involved them in an inclusion program where they would interact in a regular education class appropriate for them. Classes mainly included music, art and physical education, but occasionally the academic classes. We sought approval for this program during their admission, review, and dismissal (ARD) meeting and document the classes in the individual education plan for each student.

Each week a speech therapist came to work with the students. My assistants and I worked alongside of the individual to learn so we could incorporate the speech goals along with our other goals throughout the week. We would document the goals at the ARD meeting.

As for myself, I took thirty minutes for lunch and usually ate in the teacher's lounge. There were days I would take refuge in my van and spend the time reading. I also was allotted a forty five minute planning period, where I would sit at my desk documenting activity or filling out reports. During these times my assistants carried on with our regular schedule.

Over an eleven year period of teaching I had autistic students ranging in age from three to twelve years old. I'm grateful I had the opportunity to teach each and every one of them.

CHAPTER 13
MOVING TO RETIREMENT

AT THE END OF THE 2010 TO 2011 school year the District offered incentive packages for teachers to resign or retire at the end of the regular school year. The packages were worth up to $10,000. I choose not to take the package and later told my principal, Ms. Gamez, I wouldn't have taken it for $100,000. In fact, if I had been offered a million dollars I would have prayed to God to help me resist the temptation. At times I imagined the DISD actually offering me the million dollar package so I could smile and politely request they deposit the package where the sun doesn't shine. Of course, a full scale battle would have ensued with Joanne.

Even though I was 67 years old, I did not want to retire. I felt good about what I was doing to help others. I was in a great school with an excellent principal and staff, and to be truthful I needed the kids as much as they needed me. I thought as long as I was still an active teacher, I would not grow old. Well, times do change, so now I am faced with the reality that I have become a senior citizen. I'm just happy I have been able to write this book, which had been an obsession for me. I would also like to think of the book as a sacred mission, one I knew I must carry out.

The kids kept me young and energetic. I think back to my days as a railroad man. I was employed at the Texas Pacific Railway in Dallas from 1969 to 1971. Most men began working at the railroad when they were still teenagers and stayed until they retired at age 65. Back then, it was a reputable place to work with good pay and benefits for future security. Unfortunately, most of them died within just a few years after retirement. I guess they had a hard time adjusting from a full active and productive life to sitting on the sidelines watching the world go by in slow motion. I remember how the men would say they planned to do a lot of fishing when they retired. I think they ended up watching more television with a cold beer rather than tugging in fish on a hot day.

When I was at Mobil Oil, they paid for a retirement seminar for each retiree and their spouse so they could learn how to live a happy retired life. This benefit wasn't available at the railroad, but maybe if the program had been offered some of the old timers would still be alive with pole in hand. As such, the program would have been welcomed by their wives who became widows. One of my Mobil Oil friends, Dalton, who attended the seminar with his wife, told me many of the ladies were nervous about their husbands retiring and being home all the time.

When I was at Mobil, my desire was to retire early. I remember a discussion I had with my boss Don "Bear" Fry about my retiring when I was 55 years old. He warned me there would be a large monthly reduction if I retired early. Of course, when they forced me out at 48 years of age, I no longer had to worry about the reduction. When teaching the thought of retiring never entered my mind. But, once again the decision was made for me to leave. I still feel I was young at heart even though I almost 68 years old. Gosh, seems both Mobil Oil and the DISD took attentive care of me, no matter what my desires were. Bob Hope used to sing, "Thanks for the memories-a million thanks to you."

SO LONG RESOURCE INCLUSION PROGRAM

Late in the 2010 to 2011 school year after the district ended the incentive packages, I learned through the grapevine that my class was going to be closed at the end of the school year. When I asked my principal, Ms. Gamez, about what I heard, she said she had been told the autism class would move, but not my inclusion class. However, she assured me she would look into the situation and get back with me. In a few days, she told me what I heard was true, but that she wanted to keep the class and would speak to her supervisor. I told her if necessary I would cut back and teach half days, which would save the district half my annual salary. My main goal was to stay at Ben Milam at least one more year so I could help the four fourth grade students I was presently teaching attend fifth grade at Milam before they went on to middle school. I just wanted them to complete elementary school at Ben Milam before moving on to middle school.

Ms. Gamez met with her supervisor and fully explained our situation. She also related how a brother and sister would have to go to a different school. The girl had been in the special education program for two years and her brother had just entered at the beginning of the semester. Apparently, the administrators making the money saving decisions didn't care about kids or families, because the answer was a simple no without any explanation.

Later, we learned the same decision was forced upon the schools with less than seven students on the current role returning. No consideration was given to the students coming in from other districts or students who might qualify to be placed in special education. Once they closed the resource inclusion program, no student would dare enter special education, because they would be forced to move to another school. We attempted to point out the fact, but the administrators didn't seem to care. The unstated response to us and the effected families was, "Welcome to the DISD."

MY RETIREMENT

I was placed in the excess employee pool and in late October I was given two choices. My first choice was to leave in October, but continue to be paid through January 31. The second choice was to accept an assignment in another school as a permanent substitute while finishing out the current school year. My contract would not be renewed for the next school year. I told my principal about my decision to retire. When she notified someone (I do not know whom), he told her to have me come right down to the Administrative Building on Ross Avenue. I went there and completed the paperwork to retire. A lady helping me just told me to read the various papers and then showed me where to sign. When we were finished, she told me I was immediately free to leave the DISD and would be paid until January 31, 2012, which would be my retirement date.

I went back to Milam for the rest of that day and stayed home the following days on Tuesday and Wednesday to prepare my office and storage area for all the items I would bring home. Thursday and Friday I went back to Milam and spent the entire time packing things and giving away most of my personal furniture and learning items. I wanted to bless teachers, assistants, cafeteria staff, the custodian, the librarian, and our school crossing guard any way I could. Some of the items I had possessed for many years, but I was more than happy to see them go, especially knowing they would be used by my good friends to benefit children in the future.

My last day was, October 28, 2011. It was a very emotional day. Around seven o'clock that evening while Joanne and I were having dinner, I received a telephone call from the DISD personnel office. The lady asked if I had checked my school email. I told her I checked it when I left school for the day. She informed me that the district had sent me and the others involved an email about five thirty that afternoon assigning us to a new school on Monday. I was very upset because I had already completed the retirement papers. It appeared to be an underhanded way to notified everyone considering the email was sent after school hours on a Friday afternoon. But hey, Welcome to the DISD!

After giving away all my things plus physically moving a lot of it myself to other teachers' classrooms, I was physically and emotionally drained. I angrily told the lady who telephoned that they were going to hear from every lawyer in Dallas. However, this was just an idle threat because interestingly enough within the incentive package was a form I was required to sign which stated I would not sue the DISD under any circumstance.

I had researched the legal aspects of special education on the internet and at one time really wanted to alert the Federal government and let them know how federal laws were being broken at the DISD. After a cooling off, I thought differently, knowing what a simple teacher had to say would not get very far. My experience over the years taught me that no one in the DISD hierarchy or the

Federal Government really paid much attention to or seemed to care what the teachers down in the trenches had to say. If only the parents would pick up the cause and wage the battle, just maybe someone would be more willing to listen.

Everything had happened so fast. No one I spoke to knew if just Milam was involved in sending special education students to other schools or if there were other places of education involved in the districts sinister plan. Later I learned that there were a total of seven schools involved. It could be said that taking the incentive package was the easy way out, but I believe looking back it was the realistic way out given my attitude after all that had transpired. As I told a few of my teacher friends, "The plane is fixing to crash, and all I can do is bail out." I told them I was sorry, but it was better for me to leave than crash with the plane.

I really felt sad about leaving my students, school, and profession. Teaching was the most worthwhile job I ever had. It was my privilege to be special education teacher. I had and will always have a great deal of pride knowing I helped numerous children live better lives.

JOANNE'S RETIREMENT

Joanne taught six years at three different schools. In special education, teachers move to other schools much more than regular education teachers do. For example, I read about a regular education teacher who taught in Dallas, in the same room, at the same grade her entire thirty year career. Today, most teachers change from grade to grade, but even if they remain in the same grade they are given new rooms.

Joanne was teaching severely disabled students at City Park School when she learned the district would be reassigning her and the class to Kennedy Learning Center at the beginning of the next school year. About a week before school was to begin, we loaded her things from City Park Elementary into my van and drove over to the Kennedy Learning Center. She wanted to have her room set up early so she would be ready the first day of school.

We located the custodian and he directed us to the Development Center Classroom. However, upon arrival there was a young man in the room who told us he was the new teacher. He asked us if he could be of help. Joanne and I looked at each other in disbelief and asked if he had received a letter confirming such. He said yes, and that's when we knew that Joanne had been duped or you could say double crossed.

Verbally telling Joanne that she was assigned to Kennedy then giving the class to a new AC teacher was a typical backhanded way the district operated. We had returned home intending to call the district when the phone rang. It was the principal from Pleasant Grove, which was located on the far side of town; he asked for Joanne and informed her he had just gotten notice that she had been reassigned to his school.

We were not happy and decided it was time for Joanne to retire. Joanne was not a yes person and over the years had been outspoken about the DISD handling of various affairs. Many in the district office would be happy to see her move on. For principle sake, the decision for her to retire was probably not the smartest decision because retirement is exactly what they wanted.

I've read that 50% of teachers quit or resign within the first five years. Others teaching past five years do not make a decision to leave strictly on their own accord. DISD reminds me of a war zone with a "hit list." There are many casualties resulting from the list and in recent years teachers have the highest casualty rate. Unfortunately, school administrators make up too small a percentage on the selected "hit list." Welcome to the DISD.

MY 3 MINUTES OF FAME

After I left Gooch I had an opportunity to speak at the school board meeting that was held on November, 11, 2011. I had made the necessary arrangements and gained permission to speak a few days in advance of the meeting. Our union had instructed all interested parties how to go about gaining permission. My presentation is shown in the introduction.

Joanne who is very familiar with the DISD said it wouldn't do any good. I knew she was right, but I felt that I had to speak out. I had only three minutes, so my challenge was to say everything I needed to in that length of time. I practiced and timed myself over and over so I would not be cut off before I said all that I had prepared.

Upon arrival we sat in the last row and Ms. Rena Horea, the President of the Alliance Teachers Union, came up behind us and we spoke briefly. I was able to give her a copy of my presentation, which she included on the union website. There were probably at least one hundred teachers present. But, I was the only teacher who had requested to speak. To this day, I do not understand why I was the only teacher who spoke.

Although my presentation didn't appear to do much good, I will always feel good about my standing up to protest the malicious and morally wrong actions that were committed by the DISD against teachers, students, and their families during my teaching tenure. The DISD blamed their actions on the State of Texas for the many severe funding cuts. The cuts were real, but as I have attempted to show throughout this book, the cuts were only part of the problem at the DISD.

Joanne and I left before the meeting was over. I did have opportunity to speak with two high school teachers in the parking lot who followed us out. I regret having left early because I missed visiting with the other teachers present. This caused me regret and I felt somewhat numb on the drive home.

Leaving my teaching career was a totally different experience than when I left the military. Two extremes you might say. Stepping out of the military I felt total merriment. I was at the Tacoma Air Force Base in Tacoma, Washington, in July of 1967. My friend, Emery Ballard from Amarillo, Texas, and I had traveled together from Viet Nam to the base and spent three days processing out of the military. Once we were officially discharged, Emery and I headed for the barracks to get our things and to secure a ride to the airport. We skipped the whole way, hopping, hollering, and celebrating.

Leaving teaching created a void in my life. I wasn't prepared for all the events leading up to my retirement. Unfortunately, they were beyond my control. I was left with a deep feeling of sadness both for myself and for my students.

CHAPTER 14
CURRENT STATE OF ADMINISTRATION

In view the situation surrounding my departure one could liken it to a Greek Tragedy. I am sure some of the administrators I have dealt with over the years would call it poetic justice. We live in a free country, and they are entitled to their opinion, however I am entitled to mine as well and thus the reason for expressing some of my views and beliefs in this book.

Personally, I know I still have one heck of a lot to learn. For this reason, I always told my students a person needs to keep on learning no matter how old he or she is. I hope all adults will agree with me, especially those in charge of directing our student's education. As my experience in teaching revealed, there will always be those who will disagree. If so, please send me a copy of your book and I will be glad to read with hopes to learn something new.

Throughout my career I felt the DISD administration attempted and for the most part did a much better job in attracting and keeping good principals. Prior to my entrance to teaching this wasn't always the case. I remember an incident which had a disappointed effect on my wife, Joanne. She was a substitute teacher at the time. When one of the schools had a teacher resign, they asked Joanne to substitute until they could find a replacement. At the school where she was assigned it was common knowledge that the principal liked to frequently walk to his car and smoke a cigarette. Obviously not setting a good example, the kids who witnessed him leaving would say, "There goes Dr. Smith to have a smoke." Upon his return he would remain in his office until school let out.

It is worth noting, that in our present system, his smoking would have been a violation of school policy. For the past several years smoking has not been allowed anywhere on school property. Joanne and I surmised that he was just killing time until his retirement, which was set for the next year. Joanne was told that at one time he had been a high school principal. Therefore, he either requested to be moved to grade school or had been demoted. Principals normally went from grade school, to middle school, and then on to high school. If he had been demoted there would not have been much motivation to finish strong. The overall school suffered as a result of his lack of enthusiasm.

Teachers and principals can get tired or completely worn out after a number of years. I believe that some of our present administrators at one time could have been categorized as burned out. It is possible they entered their current administrative roles because they no longer desired to work directly with students or because they could make more money and not have to work with a single student. Granted, they work more days in the year than a teacher, but those days are usually spent shuffling paperwork, which we know takes a lot of time.

It is not my intention to be negative toward all administrators, because some are obviously needed. However, the fact remains, we have too many. Joe, a good friend who is a retired Dallas lawyer, summed up our current administrator dilemma when he said, "From what I glean from reading the Dallas Morning News the DISD has too many chiefs and not enough Indians." To which I replied, "Bingo and don't forget the big bucks they are being paid." Joe and I are in agreement that it doesn't take a rocket scientist to determine where we need to begin if we desire to improve our education system. He and I don't have all the answers to what needs to be done, but the administrative dilemma clearly stands out to me because I've seen these follies get much worse and more wasteful over the years.

When I first began my teaching career there was fewer administrators. The interesting fact was that most of them attempted to help rather than hinder teacher efforts. Unfortunately, as a result of our Uncle Sam's involvement our present system has suffered tremendously.

Let me cite a comparison between our Uncle Sam and a man I once knew in California. The man was married, kind, had a good job, did a lot for his community and overall cared about those around him. There was just one problem; he suffered with a gambling addiction. His addiction eventually placed a heavy burden on his family. Due to his inability to pay off his debts he could no longer properly support his family. The gangsters were the only people who prospered.

Our Uncle Sam, for the most part, is a kind entity who does a lot of good and cares deeply for us citizens. However, the money and resources have been foolishly depleted over the years. Thus, the only people who have prospered in our current school system are the excess number of administrators that have been hired to monitor Uncle Sam's involvement. Akin to the man's family, the rest of us along with our students, have suffered tremendously over the years.

Until recently, the DISD was doing a much better job of selecting principals, but the present selection of principals has become more complicated. During the 2011-2012 school year the new Superintendent, Mike Miles, initiated a yearlong course to train new principals. The first 57 trainees were in a program called Leadership Development Fellows Academy. They each received $60,000 for the year and had to agree to stay in the system for two years.

Unfortunately, the program was complicated in the sense, that for new principals to enter the program, existing principles had to be run off. Sixty eight principals were put on "growth plans," which identified their weaknesses, proposed remedies, and a deadline was set for improvement. As a result, about half of the principal's contracts were not renewed.

Many people in Dallas had an opinion about the process. There were two completely different trains of thought, one positive and the other negative. Some believed Mike Miles intended to replace bad principals with good ones in order to improve schools and help the students. The naysayers claim his tactics are a political motivated and designed to, among other things, bring in his "yes people." Regardless of the real reason, there was the possibility of losing good principles in the process.

I understand that this same type of training for future principals had been done in other US cities, so Mr. Miles wasn't the first to invent an in-house leadership academy. However, over the years I have witnessed many fiascos and sheer disasters involving Dallas School Superintendents. Thus, my opinion of the method by which the program was initiated will continue to be, "time will tell."

Earlier in the book I shared how Jeremy and I had swapped jobs. Had I remained in autism at that specific time in my career I believe the vast amount of documentation and the revolving door of autism administrators would have brought about my leaving on my own or possibly even my being dismissed. More than likely I would have been out of teaching in the DISD five to eight years earlier. The problem areas for me at Milam were never the students, parents, principals, teachers, therapists, or staff. Administration presented the biggest problem and so it was in the DISD. I've saw the problems escalate over time. I do not know what the future holds, but hopefully, the DISD will get better.

CHAPTER 15
GENERAL COMMENTS ABOUT OUR SCHOOL SYSTEM

Wasteful spending is a very complicated situation that needs to be studied fully and the appropriate action taken. It is time that we address the time and money wasted on many of our programs and administrators. There is a need to simplify our current Rube Goldberg (American cartoonist) type of system. Considering the complexity and interactivity of our current educational topics, both for the short term and for longer time periods, constructive planning must be carefully considered and proper timely action taken.

A good first step would be to look at the most successful school systems in our country and in other countries. Copying other districts or countries might be hard for some, because they would have to admit those districts and countries are doing a better job educating their young. However, there is no time like the present for initiating change.

Much of the responsibility rests with our Federal Government. As long as the government is throwing money at our school districts, the longer the waste will continue. I liken this to the U.S. sailors in Nha Trang referred to in the first chapter. As long as they were willing to socialize and spend money in the local bars, the bar owners were going to stay open. Thus, our servicemen were contributing to the further demise of the city. Don't you know when we pulled out of Vietnam most of those bars closed? Do you really think the North Vietnamese soldiers or the Viet Cong had the time, money, or desire to keep the barstools warm?

Let's review three areas that have been implemented in our current system, which are good, but have flaws. All of which need to be addressed by adequate and constructive planning.

The first area I want to address is our charter schools. I realize that many of these schools are very good and have true success stories to show for their efforts. The unfortunate fact is that these schools are not capable of working with special education students, especially the severely disabled. The current set up allows these schools, to a large extent, to pick and choose their students, thus helping them to be more successful. Seemingly a step in the right direction, but also a step in the wrong direction, let me explain.

Considering we continue to get more charter schools, let's brainstorm about the future of all our students. Assume for a moment that thirty years from now all we have are charter schools and no regular schools. What happens to the special education students? No problem we just take a step backward. We revert back to the way the system was set up fifty or sixty years ago and send them to big special education schools. Some of you reading this might be red in the face while accusing me of being facetious. You would be right, I am being somewhat facetious.

Allow me to share a true story about my brother. You know the one who was Down syndrome and died at twenty seven years old two days before I married Joanne. About fifty years ago, Joe went to school for the first time--he was eight years old. He lived with my parents in Jennings, Missouri, but was bused to a large County Education School for the disabled. There was no place for him in the regular schools at the time.

My point being, I agree that there are some good charter schools, but they have limitations. There needs to be more planning and regulation for these schools. More students in private schools are transferring to charter schools so they can receive public funding. For example, students in a Catholic school receive no public funding, but when they transfer to charter schools, they receive public funding. This puts enormous pressure on the current system.

There needs to be adequate planning for the public funding and many other considerations for these students. Let's assure that we get the best possible results from the charter schools without hurting any of our students. Currently the charter schools are good, but let's not compare them to the goose that lays the golden egg-just my humble opinion.

The second area I want us to look at is home schooling. There are advantages such as, students who are not in a group can move forward at their own pace. However there are disadvantages such as students losing out on social learning opportunities. Those social interactions are both negative and positive and help the students learn what it is like in the real world.

Home schooling is growing, but not as fast as the charter schools. Personally, I am not an expert on home schooling. I can only assume that parents opt for this program because they are dedicated to making schooling a success for their family. Who can blame them? Although home schooling appears to be successful for many, I think only time will tell whether the program is successful overall or will expose beneficial elements that are lacking in many of the preferred goal areas.

The third area for us to review is virtual schooling. I experienced virtual schooling when taking a graduate accounting course at the University of Dallas. I was in the regular school class, but there were a few corporate groups enrolled who were attending virtually from their offices. A camera and speakers were set up so they could see the instructor and we could hear the questions they asked the instructor. The system appeared to be very simplistic, and the students attending were all adults.

Proponents of the virtual school say the system requires far fewer teachers and saves money. As technology continues to improve, virtual schooling will probably increase and become more manageable and beneficial. The question I want us to ponder is, "How soon can an effective system be implemented for all areas and on what scale? Of course, the major unknown, should be addressed first is, "How successful will the system be overall?" We must consider the average, below average, and special education student. I am of the mind that a virtual class could be beneficial for some disabled students, but would be near impossible and costly to monitor individual educational goals. I think we can all agree there are many unknowns about virtual schooling, which should be addressed at this time.

Before further considering the future of our educational systems, let us take a glimpse into the past. I would like to share a list of 25 statistics for the year 1900 that was given to me by my good friend Walter Hydick. But, first let me tell you how I met Walter 35 years ago.

There were a total of four gun shows held each year at Market Hall in Dallas. Each year Walter traveled to Dallas and set up a booth. I was visiting one of the shows and had brought a cloth German army hat that I bought at a local pawn shop for $10. Walter, like me, was a collector of World War II items so I approached his table and asked if he could tell me if the hat was authentic. He informed me the hat wasn't authentic and then went on to show me how he determined it was a reproduction.

A few years later I purchased my own table at the shows. Market Hall was close to downtown Dallas and had hundreds of tables. I displayed, sold, bought, and traded military collectable items; especially WW II items.

When Joanne and I first dated I took her to one of the shows and she met Walter. In time Joanne and I became good friends with Walter and his wife Shirley. We learned that Walter had joined the Marine Corps at age 16 and served in China at the end of WW II. Upon returning to the states he studied art on the G.I. Bill. He and his wife were living in Los Angeles and he took a job as an artist for Walt Disney. After the birth of their first child, they moved back to his home town of Buffalo, New York. Walter passed away at the age of 84.

I was truly sorry about Walter's passing, but I'm happy he had a full and good life and that he was my friend for many years. He painted beautiful pictures during his life and I will always treasure the picture Walter painted of wild turkeys under trees covered with snow. It's hanging right above my stepson's bed, and I always admire it when I go to his condo.

The following are the 25 statistics Walter compiled about our county for the year 1900 along with my comments that came to mind as I read through the list. I also added Walter's own comments on numbers 11, 13, and 21.

1. The average life expectancy in the US was 47 years old.

Judging from the current life expectancy of 78.7 years there has been a great increase. I assume that it will keep increasing in the future, which is both good and bad. It's good that people will live longer and healthier lives. But, there will be many more people to feed and provide health care for.

I would ask these questions. What will be the nature of future wars, and are they going to be on a larger scale of destruction? How are the richer countries going to help the poorer countries? How will health care costs for older people increase and how will they be paid? Longer range questions might include. How will space exploration development effect earth residents? Will the average life span reach one hundred years old? How many present countries will be divided, merged, or conquered? What effect will the rapid technology advancement have on the world's population?

Of course, these questions address just a few of the potential considerations that might affect us and future generations. If future life expectancy continues at the current rate, there could be a drastic direct and indirect effect on everyone.

2. Only 14 percent of the homes in the US had a bathtub.

It would be interesting to know how many had running water. I would assume it was probably more common to have running water in the city than in the country.

My Uncle Bill and Aunt Rose had a farm near New Douglas, Illinois and I really liked visiting them. We would stay the whole day and I would climb in the hay loft, walk the fields up to the railroad tracks, gather the chicken eggs, climb trees, and shoot my BB gun. I enjoyed looking at the cows, pigs, geese, chickens, cats, dogs, and wild bees that had a nest above the back porch. One thing that I didn't like was the outhouse, which was located about twenty to thirty yards behind the house. They had no running water so they got their water from a well right outside the kitchen door.

They installed indoor plumbing when I was a teenager. I am glad, for their sake that they did. They lived on that farm until they were elderly and eventually moved into a senior citizens home. They did not have any children, so I do not know what happened to their old farmhouse and land. I assume they sold it when they moved. The last time I was there was when I was on leave before I went to Vietnam. I went with my parents and wife. It was Anna Marie's only time to visit there, but I'm glad she got to meet my aunt and uncle.

3. Only 8 percent of the homes had a telephone. A three minute call from Denver to New York cost eleven dollars.

When I was a boy, I liked to read comic strips in the Sunday newspaper. I remember thinking how cool it was that Dick Tracy had a 2-Way Wrist Radio, which obviously was not common at the time. Little did I know that one day we would be capable of the same technology and much more. Today, most children have their own cell phone.

Considering how far technology has advanced since I was a child, I believe it is safe to assume, technology will continue to advance at even a faster pace in the future. One might say, "Wow, isn't it great we are making such progress." But I challenge, "Are we not also getting closer to destructive types of technology?"

Thinking about nuclear weapons that are spreading to more countries around the world takes me back to my grade school religion class at St. Edwards. All the nuns would tell us how the world would eventually end with a giant fireball. Just maybe those wise nuns knew something the rest of us didn't. Now some people are addressing the same theory with an awed sense of both curiosity and dread.

4. There were only 8,000 cars in the US and only 144 miles of paved roads.

It is a historic fact that Mr. Henry Ford would provide the catalyst for these figures to drastically increase. By mass producing the Ford automobile, he made cars cheap enough for the average person. Eventually more and better roads were necessary for the amount of cars being purchased.

Another positive result was more workers were needed, which brought about an expanded economy. Development in the U.S. spread rapidly and we became one of the most prosperous countries in the world. Inventors and entrepreneurs were free to pursue their ideas and we all benefited greatly. Their success had a snowball effect, thus one of the major reasons our country grew so fast in the early twentieth century.

5. The maximum speed limit in most cities was 10 mph.

Ten mph was probably the speed that a horse and buggy traveled. There were a lot more horse and buggies than automobiles at the time, so I am sure the limit was set to facilitate an even pace of movement. Even at 10 mph, I've read that there were a lot of accidents involving cars hitting pedestrians, horses, and buggies. I assume the accidents could be blamed on driver inexperience, speeding, road congestion, bad lighting at night, and the fact that horses were fearful of the newfangled invention. People were learning by trial and error and I'm guessing some of the younger hot shots goosed their "Tin Lizzie" (nickname for the Ford Model T) up to 20 or 25 miles an hour.

6. **Alabama, Mississippi, Iowa, and Tennessee were each more heavily populated than California. With a mere 1.4 million residents, California was only the 21st most populous state in the Union.**

As more cars were produced people were able to travel and take advantage of the opportunities available in other areas of the country. Some moved out of desperation, like the people who escaped the great dust bowl in Oklahoma in the 1930's. The Okies suffered terribly, but their descendants, in general, did quite well in California.

7. **The tallest structure in the world was the Eiffel Tower.**

Years ago, I visited the Eiffel Tower in Paris and learned the structure was the tallest in the world at one time. Having just two days in Paris, I only viewed the structure from the ground, so the fact came as a surprise to me. I'm sure that if I had gone to the top, I might have gotten a better perspective and would have agreed.

Oh well, I probably won't get the chance because I doubt Joanne and I will ever go back to Paris, being such a sophisticated city, there are far too many "fancy pants" for us. For instance, during our travels we go on tours and when the guide takes the group to a restaurant Joanne and I will go for a walk. We buy some cheese, bread, and fruit from a local store and find a bench to sit on. The two of us are content to sit on the bench, eat our lunch, enjoy a nice conversation, and people watch. Inevitably, we get a kick out of hearing the group complain about waiting in a long line for the privilege to purchase a sandwich or bowl of soup for several dollars. Unknown to our fellow tour members, the guides are selective in the places they take tourists. There are no "local yokels" in those places and the people running the cash registers keep them ringing to the sound of a pleasant currency melody.

8. **The average U.S. worker made between $200 and $400 per year.**

There were a large percent of people in the U.S. living on farms so I would like to know how they fit into this category. I would think that a farming family with chickens, eggs, garden vegetables, fruit and meat from their animals would have done better on $200 a year than the folks living in the cities. The statistic would be more meaningful if the average wage was broken down into more meaningful categories.

9. **The average wage in the US was 22 cents an hour.**

I was shocked by the rate quoted, because sixty years later when I landed my first job at the hospital, I was only making seventy five cents an hour. I look at how much prices have increased up to now and think how inflation will affect prices in the future. Some say inflation is okay because our wages also increase. I believe this was truer statement in the past than it is now. The middle class and lower income people are getting further behind all the time, so I think inflation is especially going to hurt them.

10. **A competent accountant could expect to earn $2,000 per year, a dentist $2,500 per year, a veterinarian between $1,500 and $4,000 per year, and a mechanical engineer about $5,000 per year.**

I know the amounts above were big time money at that period in time. My dad, who worked many years later, never made $10,000 a year. Joanne and I still smile about the time we met my mom and her lady friend in Las Vegas, and they won $10,000 each on a slot machine at the Four Queens. We think Dad must have rolled over in his grave because he couldn't tap any of it.

When we arrived in Las Vegas, Joanne and I met my mom and her friend Dorothy at the Four Queens where they were staying. My mom wanted us to go to a sales presentation, so we would receive a voucher for a free meal. I told my mom I had been sitting all day in the airport and on an airplane. I suggested we go the next day and everyone agreed. We walked through the Four Queens and saw one very large slot machine that had five seats with everyone playing the same roll. The lady employee would pull the gigantic handle after everyone inserted his or her dollar.

I sat down along with mom and her friend while Joanne watched. The action quickly grew too slow for me, so I got up to play blackjack. When I got up, three other elderly ladies sat down and filled the remaining seats. I had just started playing blackjack when the guy sitting next to me exclaimed, "Those old gals just won $10,000 each!" I looked up and said, "Those old gals are with me!" He said, "Yea sure, you wish."

The lady who was pulling the handle told me the machine paid off every four to six weeks. My mom had made more in fifteen minutes than my dad made working a whole year. Mom was a very religious Catholic and I don't know who the patron saint of gambling was, but that night I think that holy person took care of her. Her friend Dorothy, who also won $10,000, was also a devout person. I don't know if the other three ladies had any religion, but I think in a casino everyone should practice a little piety.

I'm sure my dad would have considered $10,000 a fortune, considering that he received $35 a week in unemployment during most of the winter months, when he couldn't do cement work. He was able to buy food and gas for the car, but everything else had to wait until spring.

11. More than 95 percent of all births in the US took place at home.

I do not know where my mom was born, but my dad was born at home in 1917. His mother died during child birth. His father took him and his two sisters, aged three and five years old, to live with his mother. She raised the three children until they left as young adults to go on their own. His father never remarried, and I believe he lived a very unhappy life. When I was a boy about nine years old I remember him being in Homer Phillips City Hospital in St. Louis. My parents would go into the hospital to visit him, and I would have to wait in the car because at that time children could not visit the patients. I remember I always kept an eye out to see him at the window because he would wave at me.

He died at sixty four years old. He and his three children would have had a much more complete and happier life if my dad's mother would not have died giving birth. I think a lot of ladies died back then when having children. At the present time, under the same medical circumstances, many ladies, who would have died in the past, are now saved, which in turn affects the lives of many others in multiple positive ways. Unfortunately, in some third world countries the present death rate for women giving birth is high. The death rate for small children is also high.

Walter said that he was born at his family's home in Buffalo, New York in 1928.

12. Ninety percent of US physicians did not have a college education. Instead, they attended medical schools, many of which were condemned in the press and by the government as substandard.

Even when I was a boy, we lived in a much simpler time, and I think the nature of this statistic applied to most professions. I can think of one example.

When I was at the St. Louis College of Pharmacy after graduating from high school, the program went up to five years. Before that it was only a four year program. When my stepdaughter graduated several years ago, she had to go seven years. She was required to get a Doctors Degree to be a pharmacist. In regard to this statistic, I think the nature of the beast is only going to get hairier in the future.

13. Sugar cost four cents a pound. Eggs were fourteen cents a dozen. Coffee cost fifteen cents a pound.

In the 1950's, I remember that a haircut for males cost one dollar at the corner barber shop on Clara and Wabada Avenue. I don't think many people even tipped back then. Two brothers named John and Red (I never did know his real name, but he had red hair.) owned it. Now a haircut costs a lot more. I only pay $12.00 to a good old time barber in an ancient shop. However, we all know a haircut can cost up to $75.00 or even more plus the expected tip. The question now is how much will it cost in the future? Looking at these sugar and egg prices, haircuts could cost $300 or more.

I believe the cost of education will definitely increase drastically and we need to start now to make sure we use each dollar wisely. We can't continue to throw money into the wind and hope it lands in the small circle of wisdom rather than in the larger circle of kiss it good bye.

These prices back then might sound cheap, but considering how much the average person earned, they were expensive. At the time, the average lady of the house did not work. A lot of them, even in the city, had gardens to grow food, and they did a lot of their own canning for the winter months. I remember helping my mom can peaches, tomatoes, onions, cucumbers, and various jellies. The first half hour was fun, but the rest of the time before we were finally finished, turned to anguish. One of the most enjoyable things I remember is when we went into the woods and picked wild blackberries. I helped my mom make blackberry jelly.

Walter said that when he found a penny he would spend ten minutes at the candy store deciding which candy would give him the most for his money.

14. Most women washed their hair only once a month using borax or egg yolks for shampoo.

I remember having a flattop haircut when I was a young boy until after I graduated from high school. My friend Jerry Rose had beautiful long brown hair combed straight back. He encouraged me to grow my hair long and taught me how to comb it using Brylcream; a white cream sold in a tube and used for holding hair in place. I went from being a farm boy with little hair under my straw hat to being an Elvis protégé with long slicked hair glued back, thanks to my friend Jerry!

15. Canada passed a law prohibiting poor people from entering the country for any reason.

Canada was a long distance from where I lived in Missouri. The only thing I remember about Canada at that time is that some boys and men were going there during the Viet Nam War to avoid being drafted. Where I lived, few of us knew much less thought about escaping to Canada.

For that matter we didn't know you could join the National Guard to get out of the regular military service. I think whoever came up with the expression, "They must have just fallen off the turnip truck," was talking about me and everyone else I was acquainted with. I knew a lot of guys who went to Vietnam. Two boys from my high school graduation class were killed in Viet Nam.

16. The five leading causes of death in the US were:

    i.   Pneumonia and influenza

    ii. Tuberculosis

    iii. Diarrhea

    iv. Heart Disease

    v.   Stroke

When I read the history of our country, I frequently read that people died of consumption. This was very common in the old west. For example, I read once that the old western folk hero or villain to some, Doc Holiday, died of consumption. I always thought consumption meant drinking too much alcohol. Somehow, I eventually figured out that consumption was what we now call tuberculosis. The books at the time never used the word tuberculosis which spread easily in congested non-hygienic areas and was a major health problem.

I also remember reading it was a common problem in prisons and had incorrectly concluded that the prisoners must have been making their own booze and dying from alcoholism. Had that been the case, I'm sure the jail birds would have left the world with a smirk on their face. We are very fortunate that tuberculosis has been mostly eliminated around the world. Unfortunately, in a few countries such as India, there is now a drug resistant form of tuberculosis rendering the disease untreatable.

17. The American flag had 45 stars. Arizona, Oklahoma, New Mexico, Hawaii, and Alaska hadn't been admitted to the Union yet.

I remember when Hawaii and Alaska became states. Even though I was very young, I knew it was a big deal. There is some discussion now about Puerto Rico becoming a state. I've been there once and really liked it, especially the old Spanish Forts. I have no idea if it will become a state, but if it does, I'm sure the fireworks and some other things will hit the fan.

18. The population of Las Vegas, Nevada, was 30.

What an amazing statistic. I've been to Vegas several times and have stayed in Lady Luck, MGM, Circus-Circus, Monte Carlo, and a few others whose names I can't remember. My first trip to Las Vegas was in the summer of 1970.

My first wife Anna Marie and I drove our 1969 Pontiac. We didn't have a reservation and couldn't get a room, so after visiting several casinos we drove into a neighborhood and slept in the car. We visited some casinos the next morning and then drove straight through to St. Louis, Missouri, where my parents were keeping our two sons. Who would have ever thought you had to reserve a room? Everyone but us! A lot of times in life, we learn from the mistakes we make. Using this logic, I should be one of the smartest dudes ever.

Now people from around the world visit Las Vegas. It's a perfect place for people watching. For those who end up with an empty wallet, people watching is an especially good hobby until a friendly relative can wire them some more seed money.

19. Crossword puzzles, canned beer, and iced tea hadn't been invented.

I remember as a teenager canned beer did not have a pull tab. It had to be opened with a metal opener, which was commonly called a "church key." When the pull tab came out, people liked them because they were easy to use. The tabs became a problem because they turned into litter when they were frequently thrown on the ground. They were also harmful to animals. Progress continued and soon the push down tab stayed in the can; a seemingly small but important change. I think the beer barons did a heck of a job looking out for our ecology and assuring that animals continued to flourish.

Crossword puzzles, canned beer, and iced tea are minor inventions. I am sixty nine years old and I've seen a few major inventions that have affected me. The best invention was the jet airplane because it resulted in fast and cheap air travel.

When I was a boy, one of my family's favorite Sunday afternoon recreational activities was to drive to Lambert Airport in St. Louis to watch the passengers and airplanes. We would watch the TWA propeller driven planes land and take off. We enjoyed watching the people get on and off using the metal stairs they brought up to the door of the plane. Most of the men wore suits and ties, and the ladies had on nice dresses. Times sure have changed. I even remember when they had a smoking section on airplanes. Now I laugh. Did they think the smoke wasn't going to cross over to the non-smoking area?

I took my first airplane ride was when I was returning to St. Louis from my air force technical school in Amarillo. It is hard to believe when I joined the Air Force and left for basic training that I went from St. Louis, Missouri to San Antonio, Texas on a train. It was the Missouri Pacific passenger train, and the trip took about eighteen hours. My next move from San Antonio to Amarillo was via chartered bus. The Navy always stated, "Join the Navy and see the world." The Air Force should have proclaimed, "Join the Air Force and see Missouri, Arkansas, and Texas." Maybe I should have joined the Navy, but it's too late now. Still, all and all, I think it was smarter for me to join the U.S. Air Force rather than the French Foreign Legion. But honestly, that was the road not taken, so who knows.

In a manner of speaking, the jet airplane made the world a much smaller place. Bigger and faster airplanes along with much cheaper passenger fares made it possible for common folks to travel both within the U.S. and abroad to international destinations. Air freight greatly increased world commerce.

The other inventions that drastically affected me and everyone else were related to technology. Technology has not always been good to me. I remember when I worked for Mobil Oil, the personal computer came out. They were expensive and much more complex than they are now. Reports took a lot longer to do on the computer than on regular paper. I remember typing emails, especially long ones, then hitting the wrong button and all of a sudden goodbye to everything I had typed. I was just not a good technology person. Of course, there sure were a lot of young college graduates joining Mobil who could do every trick in the book on a computer.

20. There was no Mother's or Father's Days.

There were fewer holidays back then than we enjoy now and most people take our forty hour workweek for granted. In 1900 and beyond it was not uncommon for people to work ten or twelve hours a day six days a week. I understand some even worked seven days a week. They also didn't earn overtime pay as people do now. Sadly, even working long hours, they had a hard time supporting their families. It was a hard life.

But, from what I have read, it was a better life than the one many of them had in their country of origin before traveling by ship to the U.S. On both sides of my family some of my relatives have been doing genealogy research. They were kind enough to send everyone in the family the information they discovered. I was happy to receive the information, because I always wanted to know about my ancestors, but was so busy with other things that I didn't do it myself. The truth is I wouldn't even know how to go about the task. My mother's parents came from a small city in Poland, which is now part of the Ukraine, with their first born son. They had six more children after settling in St. Louis, Missouri. My father's grandfather came from a small German village near Hanover. He married a lady in St. Louis, and they had eight children.

When I was a young man, some of the leisure days we enjoy now, did not even exist. We now have Martin Luther King Day plus a few other floating holidays. I still don't think we've caught up with some of the European countries in terms of the number of holidays we celebrate. I'm not an economist, but I'm sure that for the sake of our economy, it is better that we never catch up to our sophisticated friends across the pond in regard to the number of vacation fete-days they have for celebrating. However, I'm sure we will keep trying.

On Christmas Eve, it's now common to work only a half day. On my first three jobs, I worked until 5 p.m. on Christmas Eve. While working at the Missouri Pacific in St Louis, the only Christmas cheer we had was when one of the top managers came around a few minutes before 5 p.m. to shake our hand and say, "Merry Christmas." The other employees and I appreciated his gesture; because that's the way it was everywhere.

The day after Thanksgiving is now a holiday for most. I remember the days when we all had to go to work on the Friday after Thanksgiving. As such, we had to watch just how much holiday spirit we enjoyed at our celebrations on Thursday. Sometimes, we didn't do so well and were forced to struggle through Friday the best we could. Of course, we were always ready to begin again after work and experience more fun over the weekend.

21. One in ten US adults couldn't read or write.
   Only 6 percent of all Americans had graduated from high school.

I'm curious about what the percentage is now in our country. I told you my mom went through eighth grade and my dad through fifth grade. My mom could read and write well. My dad could read, but I never saw him write anything except his name.

I've saw many sixth graders in my last school who had trouble reading. Some had great difficulty writing using correct grammar, spelling, and punctuation. The latter is especially true with some of the English as second language students.

I enjoyed teaching my students to read and write. I kept many of my own books on three bookcases in my classroom. At various times throughout the year, I would let the students choose a book or two to take home, read, and keep. I knew what type of book each student liked, so I would be on the lookout to find them, purchase them, and then bring them to school. Sometimes, I would give them books when they did good work. At other times, such as just before winter and spring break, I would let them pick out a few books. At the end of the school year, they were able to choose several books to read and enjoy over the summer.

Walter said that neither of his parents made it past sixth grade. They had to go to work.

22. Marijuana, heroin, and morphine were all available
   over the counter at corner drugstores. According to one
   pharmacist, "Heroin clears the stomach and the bowels,
   and is, in fact, a perfect guardian of health."

Earlier in the book I mentioned that I never saw or heard about drugs from the time I was in grade school through high school. Even in Vietnam I was never exposed to drugs. My tour of duty was somewhat early in the war and I spent most of my time in the

Nha Trang area, which was not like being in the big cities of Saigon or Da Nang. Granted I was not looking for any type of drug including marijuana, but if the drugs were readily available, I think I would have known.

However, later in the war, drugs became a major problem for U.S. military personnel in Vietnam. I've read that a few soldiers in the field used drugs to calm their nerves and to get some sleep. Others, in more secure areas, used drugs because they were readily available, cheap, and made the time pass quicker. Today, illegal drug usage continues to grow. It drastically affects people in our country as it does others around the world.

Some questions in regard to illegal drugs in the US might include: Are drugs other than marijuana going to be made legal in some states? If so, which ones and how will they be monitored? Will there be a large increase in the number of drug users? How will organized crime continue to benefit if drugs become legal? What will be the future laws and punishments for illegal drug use? Who will pay for the probable large increase in funding we will incur to combat drugs? How can our penal system cope with increased populations due to incarcerating more drug users?

To me the drug issue is a terrifying subject, because it affects so many people, especially young people. It also has a damaging effect on the addicted peoples' families, friends, and coworkers. It's a major concern and appears that it will get worse in the near future.

23. Eighteen percent of households in the US had at least one full-time servant or domestic.

The statistic above reveals how bad the economy really was. Many people were willing to work menial jobs for very low wages because there was no other employment. There were few social programs, such as unemployment compensation payments, to help those people who were unemployed. In view of this, a low paying job was better than nothing, especially if it included room and board.

The availability of low paying household servants still exists in many countries. I read that many citizens in the Philippines will go to other countries to work. The women work as household servants in the rich Arab countries, and the men work on ships travelling around the world.

24. There were only about 230 reported murders in the entire US.

This is the one statistic that I find very hard to believe. I would be willing to bet that many of the murders were probably never reported or if they were, record keeping was not very accurate. A lot of people had guns and the police were not as advanced as they are today. I remember when I was a boy we had a policeman walking a beat in our neighborhood on Friday and Saturday nights. He would kill two birds with one stone when he visited the taverns. He would go in to make sure everyone was all right, and then would down a beer before moving on. Back then, everyone was glad to see the dedicated policeman and felt he was doing a good job. I think if a policeman exhibited the same behavior today, someone would quickly snitch and the so called dedicated officer would be fired.

The twenty four statistics stated above show the drastic changes that have taken place in our country over the last century. The future planning for our U.S. educational system should not necessarily give priority to the next century, but should at least set the course for the next, five, ten, twenty, and even forty years. Uncle Sam and our school systems appear to be planning ahead, but I'm suggesting realistic planning. We must get away from our present methods that involve so many political decisions, which result in an unreasonable waste of funds and other valuable resources.

CHAPTER 16

HUMOROUS, RIDICULOUS, RACY, AUDACIOUS, AND PREPOSTEROUS STORIES

HELL'S BELL'S, now that I've preached doom and gloom, let's take a break and have a laugh or two. I want to tell you a few humorous, ridiculous, racy, audacious, or preposterous stories about adult related events that occurred over my teaching years. I'll tell you about one contemptible event, but I am also going to tell you a few down to earth tales. You may not think they are believable, but they are all definitely true. You have my word as a former boy scout.

❧❧❧

THE GANG BANG

When I was at Tom Gooch Elementary computer usage for teachers was just beginning, but very few autism teachers had a computer. I bought my own computer and my assistant Dicloria set it up for me in our classroom. I brought it mainly for the students to use.

We had an autism workshop and an administrative man, who was a speaker, had an idea. He told us if we wanted computers, we should approach it like a gang bang. Besides myself there were two other men and about twenty women teachers present. No one blinked an eye, but everyone listened intensely. He suggested that every time one of us saw the lady who headed special education, we should ask about receiving computers and remind her autism teachers needed computers.

We followed his advice and sure enough, a few months later, we were all told we could get a computer. Of course, in order to get one we had to pay our dues and go through a multi-step process. We were required to attend an all day Saturday computer class at E D Walker School in North Dallas. Next we had to attend two evening classes at Nolan Estes Center in Oak Cliff. We received no payment for these classes and for me it involved driving about five miles to Walker and about fifteen miles through traffic in downtown Dallas to get to Estes. Finally, we had to go to E. D. Walker to sign papers to receive the computer and then haul it to our school in our own vehicle.

Personally, I never saw the lady who was in charge of special education, so I had not participated in the noble venture our administrative friend had advised. But the gang prevailed and the computers arrived with a bang.

THE CONFRONTATION

I had three assistants while teaching at Tom Gooch Elementary. For the most part, we worked together well, and the students benefited from having four adults in the classroom. However, once in a great while, there was tension among the adults that was usually caused by stress, a crowded classroom, or difficult job tasks.

I don't fully remember what caused my assistant, Dicloria Eddington, and me to get into a dispute in our autism classroom. But, it became heated and escalated to the point that we were both tracking out of the room to go to the principal's office to let him decide who the winner of our debate was.

As we hurriedly walked down the hall, Sharon, one of my other assistants forcefully said, "Bob and Dicloria get back in this room right now!" She said it like a mother speaking to her two children, and Dicloria and I immediately returned to the room. Sharon told us in no uncertain terms we were going to solve our issue in the classroom not in the principal's office.

Later that week I saw our principal, Ron Powell, in the hall and he smiled and said, "Heard that you and Dicloria had a little discussion." There were definitely no secrets to be kept in school. Fortunately, in a few days the two of us made up and we never had another disagreement like that again. Most close friends get into an occasional dispute and it brings them closer together. Dicloria and I can laugh about it now. I have one final comment for my friend Dicloria, "Thanks for the many memories we share."

THE TACKLER

When I had my autism class at Walnut Hill Elementary, I was without an assistant for a few months. One lady would frequently substitute in my class. She had children in our school and was president of the PTA.

On most days, we would take the class to a public playground located next to the school. She stood on one end of the playground and I on the other. One sunny beautiful day, I noticed one of our somewhat mischievous students, Jack, start running toward Walnut Hill Lane. The street bordered the other side of the playground so as quick as Flash Gordon, my assistant ran after him.

Before he could reach the sidewalk she tackled him. Both rolled harmlessly on the soft ground. I was amazed. I knew she was a very good PTA president and an excellent assistant, but I didn't know she could outrun one of my students and make a perfect flying tackle.

I would like to thank Ms. Beverly Good for helping me and my students and especially for saving Jack with a tackle any college football coach would be proud of.

HAM HOCKS AND BEANS

When I was at Tom Gooch Elementary, we held birthday celebrations for the students and the adults. For the adults, we would have a 'surprise' luncheon in our room. When it was my birthday in February, Sharon would bring homemade ham hocks, beans, and corn bread, all gourmet food that I fully enjoyed. I never made ham hocks and beans so the only time I had them was when Sharon made them for my birthday. I savored those meals as any connoisseur of the cooking art would on his or her one special day of the year.

I want to thank Ms. Sharon Hawkins for being a good friend, a great assistant, and of course the best ham hocks and beans specialist in the whole USA. I say USA because I'm not sure it's made anywhere else. To Miss Sharon and all of my former assistants, "I love you."

COOKING THE BOOKS

When I began teaching, record keeping was a relatively easy task using pen and paper. Over the years keeping records has become more and more complicated especially when everything became computerized. There have been many benefits derived from computerizing, but the process still takes time. During my days in the accounting department at Mobil Oil creativity involved doing what time allowed each day and estimating what wasn't necessary to complete the report. My accounting friends jokingly stated we were, "cooking the books," but of course this was just an expression, no one actually did anything illegal or unethical.

Special education laws have also gotten more complex, almost to the point of being senseless. The large amount of time required for the teachers to do documentation and reports takes away from the time the teachers have to work with students and doing other constructive projects such as planning. There were between twelve and twenty forms required just for the annual Admission, Review, and Dismissal (ARD) meetings. Presently all forms are available on line, which has been a helpful change.

There was one report that dealt with autism students and whether they would be allowed to attend summer school. Most parents wanted their children to attend summer classes because their participation was such a positive experience for the student and family. The first several years of my teaching career determining summer attendance was a simple matter. We would put a capital E in red ink on the first page of the ARD papers indicating extended year service. However, during my first two years at Ben Milam, things drastically changed. I don't know what triggered it, but Uncle Sam determined, "Hey, it costs a lot of money to send autistic kids to summer school, so I want extensive documentation stating the students will regress if they don't attend. No proof, then they don't go." At this point, the reports were still done on paper so the teachers were required to turn them in to the autism department so they could be put into the computer system. Only then were teachers told who would be allowed to go to summer school.

Sometime later we were required to input the information on the students ourselves into the computer. On the students' Individual Education Plan, we could include twelve to twenty objective goals. At the end of each goal, we were to state how many times out of a number of attempts the student must complete the task. For example, a student might need to complete four out of five attempts or seven out of ten attempts. At the time, I had nine students so I had to document about 135 goals each day on the computer. I was spending about two hours a day doing this one report. There was just not enough time in the day so I "cooked the books." Interestingly, I found out later that some of the teachers were not logging their information. Of course, I always tried to do everything I was told, even if it was an impossible task.

A few weeks after I submitted my reports, I was down at the administrative building on Ervay Street picking up a few computer programs. The computer room was on the same floor as the autism department, so I paid a visit. One of the ladies told me I had done the best job submitting student data than any of the other teachers. However, next she also told me that not one of my students had qualified for summer school attendance. I was perplexed thinking, "The process was great for saving money, but it is bad news for my students and their families."

THE CLOSET LAPTOP

In 2003 at Ben Milam, all teachers were to be given a laptop computer. Seemingly good news, but we had to accept the computer whether we wanted one or not. For me, like I related earlier, I had a nice computer at school, and no one could steal it like they could a laptop. We were also required to take a long and tough computer test before we would be issued our computer. But, they sweet talked us by telling us we could buy the laptop after three years for a one dollar bill.

Of course, after the three years, I had to drive to the administrative building on Buckner Boulevard to spend another three hours to pay a one dollar bill to own the laptop that I kept in my closet. My laptop had a good home in that closet for about five years until I finally gave it away.

Yes, Uncle Sam had paid a lot of money for those computers so in the beginning from time to time we would get a form letter from the principal stating our jobs were at stake if we didn't complete the testing process. I'm sure the letter was passed down to the principal from the DISD administration. Unfortunately, some long tenured 'non computer savvy' teachers decided to retire.

The DISD had a course in the summer for non-geeks like me to prepare. We went for two full days and were paid $100. It was a hard course and at the end of the second day we were expected to pass a test. I had practiced on one computer for the two days, but when I took the test I was told to go into another room. To my surprise there was a totally different type of computer and I couldn't figure out how to turn it on. Thus, it came as no surprise to me that I failed the test.

I spent a lot of time studying, but knew I needed help to pass the long complicated test. Thank God I attended the Alliance Teachers Union two Friday evening computer classes at North Dallas High School. They were for union members who were lacking in computer skills. I was given material to take home to practice and study and I spent a lot of time preparing.

I went one evening after school to Greiner Middle School in Oak Cliff to take the test. The people giving the test were not very polite. They threatened us by saying anyone looking at another's work would immediately be kicked out. I spent about two hours taking the test and passed.

The next complicated step was that on a Saturday, I had to go to Estes Plaza in East Dallas to stand in line, sign papers, and get the laptop I never wanted. I would like to know how much money the pie in the sky "closet computer" giveaway cost our Uncle Sam. Sammy, I will continue to pray for you. God knows you need all the help you can get.

THE GOOCH GOLDEN LADIES

Mrs. Cruz and Mrs. Smith both substituted for my assistants many times in my autism class at Tom Gooch over a six year period. Both ladies had a lot in common. They were both at least in their seventies. Their husbands had died when they were in their sixties, so they had been widows for many years. Both ladies were patient, caring, and loving toward our students.

When I first started using Mrs. Smith, she told me she could not substitute the day I needed her because she had a water aerobics class on that day. She was too good to lose so I made an executive decision. I asked if she would be willing to come to

Ms. Smith working with a student

the school early and then leave in order to make her water class. If time allowed she could return when her class was finished. She graciously agreed, so it was a win-win situation for our students and her water aerobics pals. Oh yes, for me too.

Mrs. Cruz substituted in my class and in the regular education classes, so she was busy at Tom Gooch. One of my assistants told me that Mrs. Cruz's birthday was coming on a day she would be substituting in our class. We had a surprise party for her with cake,

Ms. Cruz with students on the playground

refreshments, and gifts. Throughout the day other staff members would come in to wish her a happy birthday. She was very surprised and happy. She thanked us at the end of the day. We then told her it was far more important that we should thank her for all she was doing for our class and school.

I have not seen either lady in the twelve years since I left Gooch, but I want to say, "Thank you and God Bless my Gooch Golden Ladies, Mrs. Alma Cruz and Mrs. Geraldine Smith, wherever you are."

TINSEL SURVEYS

During each school year, the teachers met three or four times after school to complete a survey. We did surveys about our principal's performance, our preferences for the next year's school schedule, questions about the whole school district, teacher morale, and various other subjects. Once we did the surveys, we seldom heard any more about the results. Of course we were given the next school year's schedule but it was never exactly how we voted for it.

The first several years of teaching when I took the surveys, I spent ample time choosing what I thought to be the best answer. The last several years, I just read the questions and quickly filled in the circles with my answers. I wasn't sure our answers counted for much, but it gave some administrators more information to juggle, shake around, and swirl much like a bartender making a cocktail. The only difference being, the barkeep ended up with a specific drink that was ordered, but I think the survey ended up with whatever the scorer wanted it to be.

Maybe the tinsel surveys were a good morale booster for the new teachers who were theoretically part of the decision making process. I have my doubts about any other advantages.

BABY, WEDDING, AND PUPPY SHOWERS

While I was at Tom Gooch, we had several baby and wedding showers for staff members at my house. We would have them on a Friday evening after school. I lived just several blocks from school and our house was large with a nice size den. So there was lots of room to spread out the gifts. We put out refreshments in the kitchen and everyone helped themselves. Joanne always helped get everything ready. We took photos, and everyone had a good time.

At my next school, which was Ben Milam, we always had the showers in the library or teachers' lounge. In my first year there, we had a dog shower for a staff member who just gotten a puppy. We had the usual refreshments, but the gifts were different in that they were doggy related rather than regular baby gifts. The lady staff member brought her puppy and the little canine seemed to enjoy all the attention and the fun presents.

I never knew the whole story behind the need for a puppy shower, but it was the first and only puppy shower I ever attended. I've seen some strange things in my teaching career and the puppy shower rated right up there as one of the most unusual, but interesting. It was an occasion I will always remember.

RED LEATHER HOT PANTS

At Ben Milam each December, there was a party for the school staff. We would either hold it in a restaurant, in the party room of my condo building, or at someone's home. One party I will never forget was held in one of our teacher's parents' home.

We had food catered in, and everyone brought their own wine, beer, or whatever they wanted to drink. Each person brought a wrapped gift and after eating we swapped gifts. We drew numbers to see who would go first to pick the gift they wanted. It was interesting because when it was your turn you could take the gift from the previous person and give them your number to pick again. My wife Joanne had to go to another party with her son, but she gave me a gag gift to take, a pair of lady's bright red leather hot pants.

Mrs. P picked my gift and took the hot pants gingerly out of the wrapped box. I don't know if she was surprised, shocked, or astonished, but she didn't utter a word. She had a blank look on her face. Everyone was laughing. Then the person who had the next number came up and took the hot pants from her and gave Mrs. P his number. He was a thin young man, so he put the hot pants on over his regular pants and pulled them up. Now there was uproarious laughter by everyone present. I'm glad one of our teachers was quick to pull out her telephone to take pictures. It was perfect because it recorded the event for our memoirs.

A few years latter Ben Milam had its one hundred year anniversary. My Milam staff planned a nice Saturday celebration complete with speakers, refreshments, tours of the school, and the loading of a time capsule. I don't know if the picture of the young man wearing bright red hot pants made it into the time capsule, but I think it should have. It would have definitely been a conversation piece one hundred years down the road.

I also don't know what the teacher's parents thought about our fun evening, but I hope they thought, "Teachers are definitely not as boring and unornamented as our daughter describes them to be."

BOUNTIFUL BUTCHER PAPER

Butcher paper comes in various colors in large rolls and is used as a background for school display boards. The paper I used came on a roll 3 feet wide and 1,000 feet long. In the second semester, it was used to cover anything and everything in all rooms were the state tests were given. When I taught, the students from third grade through high school were required to take the Texas Assessment of Knowledge and Skills (TAKS) test. Presently there is a different test called the State of Texas Assessments of Academic Readiness (STAAR.) These are the names of the Texas tests, but all states have because Federal law requires it.

I understood covering learning materials, but the rule makers were benumbed when they required us to cover everything such as alphabet letters and books on a shelf. At Milam, all rooms were used for testing, so every book on every shelf had to be covered. No book in our library could be seen.

It would take a psychic and gifted student to look at a book on any book shelf and determine the correct answer to a test questions, but school administrators take these tests very seriously. Every school had hall monitors throughout the school so no visitor could come in and no student could go out. Parents were sent

These two pictures show my Resource Classroom at Ben Milam
before and during the annual state tests.

Before tests...

...and during tests.

notices not to come on the test days, which were held on several different days over a period of weeks. The whole school was quiet as a cemetery until the last student finished. If students were not finished by the end of the school day, they were required to stay until they finished.

Some teachers were concerned about their safety when they had to climb ladders to cover high materials. In these cases, the principal would usually let the custodians help. I knew one teacher who took down all the high displays. They stayed down, and no others were put up. In my classroom, I covered the high displays and they stayed covered for weeks until the last test was over.

Multiply the costs of the butcher paper and the time required to measure, cut, and tape the paper up in hundreds of thousands of rooms. We're talking about some serious money, not to mention some who were impaired from falling off ladders.

But looking at it in a positive manner, I'll have to admit the rooms looked different and somewhat comely with all the draped colorful paper.

SMOKEY THE BANDIT

At my first school, the Walnut Hill staff who wanted to smoke could do so out on the back porch by the teachers' parking lot. There was an ash tray which usually held a number of cigarette butts, because several of the staff smoked.

At my next school not many of the Tom Gooch staff members smoked, but for those who did they could smoke in their car or in a designated area around the school. Smoky, our custodian would frequently smoke as he talked on his cell phone while riding the lawn mower to cut the side grass, which was outside our class window. During my last year at Gooch, DISD made a rule that smoking would not be allowed anywhere on school property, including parking lots and sidewalks. I do not know if it was true, but it was rumored that the few smokers would get their tobacco hits down in the boiler room. Sorry, Smoky, I didn't mean to spill the beans, but I think you're safe because the time limit for castigation is past.

At my third school, we initially had several smokers. They would walk across the street and smoke on the opposite sidewalk on McKinney Avenue. One brave teacher would stand on the cement median strip separating the lanes of traffic on Fitzhugh which was a busy street. This spirited lady soon retired. All of the others quit smoking rather than brave the rain, cold weather, and time restraints involved in making three or four smoke excursions a day. I guess that all good things must end.

PRINCIPALS LEARN SPANISH IN ONE WEEK

The DISD had a program for teachers to learn Spanish. We attended one evening a week for each ten week session. The class lasted two hours and was taught by a DISD teacher. We had excellent teachers, were assigned homework, did presentations, had buddy discussions with a partner in class, and met others interesting teachers who were in class. We learned a lot, and our instructors, who received a stipend, seemed to enjoy teaching us Spanish. I was able to attend four sessions. There was only one session a year, so I attended four years at Spence Middle School, North Dallas High School, and Woodrow Wilson High School. It was a very good program.

Of course in the DISD, the program was just too good to be true. The program was killed and the program funds were used to send selected principals to Mexico for one week with most expenses paid. I assume some administrative genius thought the principals could learn Spanish in one week's time.

Knowing the DISD as I do, I pose this question, "Did the administrator making that decision go along with the principals as their guru to rapid learning?" The answer is maybe or maybe not, but to this day I haven't a clue. All I know is that many of the DISD decisions did not make sense. However, they sure took away precious funds that could have been used more beneficially. That's the way it is. Welcome to the DISD!

A JOB INTERVIEW DEAD END

When my time was coming to an end at Tom Gooch, my friend PE Therapist Tommy Oakley, told me about an autism teacher job that was available at Ben Franklin Middle School in North Dallas. He told me it even paid an extra $3,000 a year because the teacher did not get a planning period.

The extra money sounded good, but the most important thing on my agenda was finding a new school for me and my assistant Barbara. I called and arranged for an interview, which was set for 3:00 p.m. the next day. I was told I would be interviewing with the assistant principal rather than the principal. I immediately became suspect thinking it odd that an assistant principal would be interviewing me. I firmly believed I should have been interviewing with the principal considering the hiring of an autism teacher is important.

The experience reminded me of a gal named Martha in Accounts Receivable when I was at Mobil Oil. When Martha felt someone had a bad attitude, she would say they had a "tude." Well, the interview did not go well at Franklin because the Assistant Principal who interviewed me had a "tude." Come to think of it I had a "tude" as well. After looking at the school and getting a feel of the school environment as the students were getting off for the day, I didn't feel this was the right fit for us anyway. Obviously, I was not offered the job and thank God because Barbara and I were fortunate to go to Ben Milam.

A lot of times when Joanne and I drive past Ben Franklin I smile and tell her, "That could have been my Alma Matter."

MARIJUANA COOKIES

For the first fifteen years I taught at all three schools, the Mothers Club would provide food at various times throughout the school year for the staff. For example, on Teacher/Parent conference nights, they would provide a good meal before the meetings began. Some of the selection was store bought, but most of the food was home made. The teachers really enjoyed this because the food was very tasty, and there were ample choices. We could get things we liked and try things we never had before or that just looked wonderful.

I don't know the exact details how, but a former high school student sneaked cookies containing marijuana into the teachers' lounge at a Dallas area high school. Some of the staff, thinking another staff member had brought them for everyone, ate the cookies. It soon made them sick. It didn't take Sherlock Holmes to figure out what happened, and the culprit was caught. I don't know what chastisement he faced but as a result of his meanness, no more homemade food could be served in the school. So the Parent/Teacher conference meal consisted of store bought pizza. One senseless act affected many people at the time and in the future.

I am reminded of the marijuana cookies every time I have to take off my shoes before going through airport security. All of us suffer because one person had an explosive in his shoe on an airplane. I read where another fellow had explosives in his underwear. I don't know for sure, but I think that may have resulted in the nude x rays. I hate to think what might happen next and even scarier what the new traveling requirements will be imposed.

THE BULLDOZER LADY WARM UP

In August of 1996, the new DISD Superintendent Yvonne Gonzales appeared to drive a bulldozer across the floor of Reunion Area to the boxing ring stage area. Approximately 19,000 DISD employees cheered as the bulldozer passed through fire and smoke.

The $50,000 back to school rally included fireworks, skits, speeches, and hip hop music done by high level administrators impersonating rock stars. One who was dressed in a black muscle shirt sang "We Will Rock You." Others impersonated big-name entertainers danced to "La Bamba," "Respect," and "Soul Man." It was a lot of showmanship and the audience was impressed and had fun.

All the schools chartered buses to take their faculty to the downtown facility, and each school had a location to sit together. I think all of us at Tom Gooch Elementary had a good day, but it got much better after we returned to school. Our principal invited us to attend a happy hour at a nearby Mexican Restaurant. The rally was good because it was a warm up for our more important happy hour, which got us ready to prepare our Gooch school house morale for another great year ahead. All of my years at Gooch were majestic and magical. We only had one bulldozer event, but that didn't stop us from having an occasional happy hour meeting even without the long-winded adventure to warm us up.

As it turned out Yvonne Gonzales was not actually driving the dozer, but there was a real bulldozer driver crouched beside her. That's okay if a lot of the pageantry was not as it seemed, because it was more of a P. T. Barnum event. Of course everyone loves a circus, and the event provided a nice memory, but it drained the district bank account of funds that could have been better utilized for the advancement of our students. A few years latter Ms. Gonzales was sent to prison for misuse of funds; she had used the funds to buy furniture for her home. Welcome to the DISD!

Ok, we've had some smiles, snickers, and some food for thought, so in the next chapter it is time to get back to a more serious train of consideration.

CHAPTER 17
CROSSING THE RIVER

C ROSSING THE RIVER is an old expression meaning to die. I remember the term best when General McArthur stated, "When I *cross the river*, my last conscious thoughts will be of the Corps." McArthur was giving his farewell speech to the students at West Point as he was nearing the end of his life.

I am going to use McArthur's expression in another terminology. I crossed the river when I retired from teaching. Being a special education teacher was the most worthwhile career I could ever hope for. I was proud of my profession and truly enjoyed working with and helping the students. I loved the creativity, my school, the students, the parents, and the Ben Milam staff. I had no desire to cross the river, but now I am across the river so I must explore what the future holds.

THIS IS WHAT I'VE DONE SO FAR:

- I've spent a good deal of time researching and writing this book. I have found it challenging but a very rewarding experience. It brings back many memories. Some of these are good and some are bad. Frankly I've found it more than challenging for many reasons. One was the digging up of some old skeletons from the past. The research to get the facts from years past took much longer than I believed it would.

- I am volunteering to work one morning a week on the Trinity Audubon Trails. We water plants, varnish benches, work on trails, dig up and plant trees and bushes, haul mulch and rocks, pick up litter, repair broken items, set up bird houses and hummingbird feeders, work on trails or the natural habitat growing on the roof of the building, and just about anything else that needs to be done. We do whatever the volunteer coordinator wants us to do or whatever we think should be done. I work with two long term volunteers who I learn a lot from. Mike and Jim are also retired, and I enjoy working with them. They are kind enough to share their vast knowledge of nature with me and to answer my various questions.

- I spend more time buying and selling items on EBay. My friend Jeremy helped us set up EBay and PayPal several years ago. Since then, I have been downsizing Joanne's and my collections of vintage toys, military collectable items, antiques, sports and Olympic collectables, and many other types of rare items. It's very time consuming, but I find it fun and a good learning experience.

- I have always read a lot, but now I have more time to read even more. I read two newspapers, the Dallas Morning News and the Wall Street Journal, approximately twenty five monthly magazines and newsletters, and four different books I keep in different places. For example, I keep one in the den, so I can read it during commercials on TV. When I go on vacation I have all the newspapers and other reading material saved, so I can read them when I return. I took a speed reading course about forty years ago, which allows me the extra time to read, I do not care much for television except for a few cable shows and some of the reality television shows.

I am addicted to reading as much as some are to their video games, or whatever they do on their phones. I do not know exactly what all they do because I have never owned a cell phone. I occasionally borrow Joanne's, but sometimes beyond making a simple telephone call she has to show me how to use it. I watched some of my teacher friends use their cell phones, and I am amazed that they could move their fingers that fast. Maybe in another life, I will have a cell phone and even be able to take photos with it.

Speaking of other lives, when I was in my mid-thirties, I went to a famous Dallas hypnotist. One of the things, we did was to go into my previous lives. In one session, I was a farmer in a small English village in 1565. My name was John York. I had a full beard, and I was thin. I was muscular and had smooth skin so I believe I was a young adult. I saw the small thatched hut I lived in and could actually smell the smoke from the cooking fire and the manure from the animals.

In another session, I was a cowboy living in a plain small room above a saloon. I was wearing boots and a flannel shirt with a vest. I could hear the piano being played loudly downstairs. My name was Will and I had curly red hair. My friend's name was Burt. My wife had died and I was living a shiftless life. I had all the money I needed and was apparently a professional gambler.

In another session, I was a professor at Heidelberg University in Germany in 1823. I was walking back to my two story home near campus. I had on glasses and was wearing a suit and nice black shoes. I had a wife, a son, and two daughters. I could see my wife who was pleasingly plump. She was wearing a fashionable dress. Unfortunately, I did not see my daughters which would have really been exciting for me because Anna Marie and I only had two sons.

In another session I was a native named Jasmain in the Amazon Jungle. I could see large beautiful trees and a river where we had canoes. I lived with a small group of other natives and we lived a communal life. We lived from fishing and hunting and waged war with other tribes. I do not remember the time period of my Amazon life.

The previous life experiences were interesting, and I could picture myself living each of those lives. I wish I could have pursued more of my past lives, but there was a lot going on in my present life that I had to focus on. I had a busy job at Mobil Oil and was running the house doing cooking, cleaning, shopping, etc. I was fortunate to have my two sons and my finance Patsye. Patsye had two children of her own and a very busy and difficult job at a large company. As deeply as we loved each other, we broke up after about three and a half years.

I still don't fully understand all the reasons for our disunion. I think there were several reasons for this, but as I think back I believe it was probably mostly my fault for not setting a specific and early wedding date. I have not seen Patsye for about thirty years. I still think of her as one of the nicest and most decent ladies, I have ever had the privilege of knowing. She was also one of the prettiest, and I would be willing to bet she still is. I wish her the best and hope she and her family had a good life and will continue to have happy lives long into the future.

- We are attending more events and going to museums and places we've been putting off for a long time. For example, we went to Love Field to see the B17 and B24 World War II airplanes which were in Dallas for a short time. It was a weekday but still crowded, so I can imagine how crowded the weekend must have been. We walked through the planes and spoke to veterans who had flown on similar planes.

  I could not have gone to see the planes if I was still working. Many social events were held on weekday evenings. For example, The Downtown Homeowners Association had frequent events. I would sometimes attend, but would decline a cocktail and leave early knowing I had to be up at 4:30 a.m. on weekday mornings.

  Previously I went to the YMCA at 5:30 a.m. to work out or to take a water aerobics class. From there, I went to my classroom to have breakfast before the day started. Now, I go to the water aerobics class and return home and go back to bed for a while. I found out that retirement does have some advantages. However, I still keep a normal busy schedule.

- I made myself an office on one side of my stepson's storeroom. Warren lives on the second floor, and I live on the ninth floor of our condo building. I brought some of my personal classroom furniture, books, and accessories home to do this. Over the years, I bought most of the furniture and learning materials that were in my classroom. Then I would give most of it away when I retired.

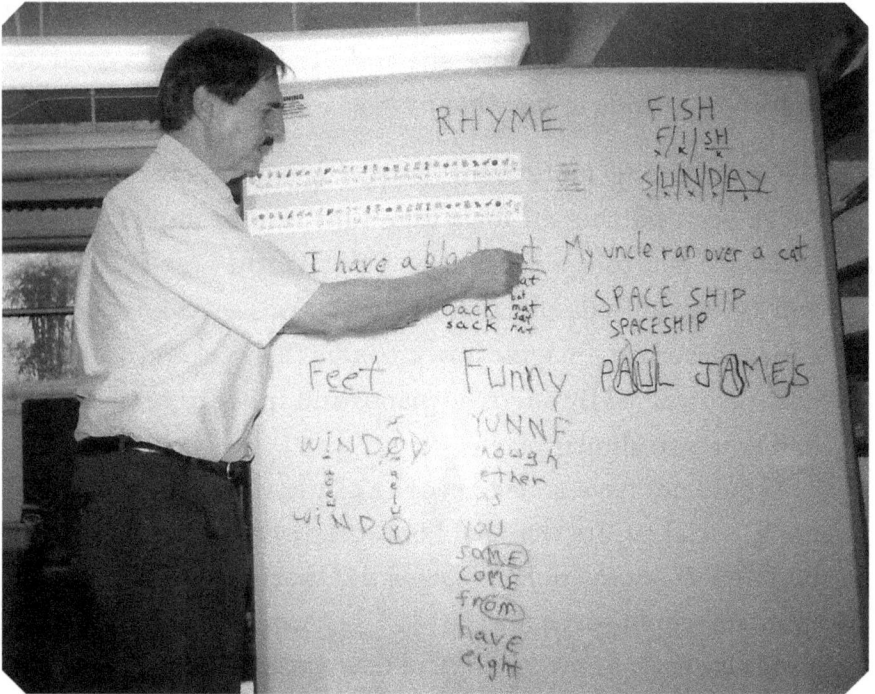

I purchased this Plexiglas light-up writing screen from a man who closed his business. The screen was a bargain at $50 because I used it for 8 years. The students loved working and learning with the medium. When I retired I gave it to another teacher.

For example, I gave my friend Karin a small end table that my friend John Alsup made in his high school woodworking class for me about fifty years ago. I also gave her a bookshelf my father-in-law made about forty years ago. I gave various teachers, librarians, assistants, cafeteria workers, and custodians books, puzzles, furniture, microwave, learning materials, wall clock, tools, Plexiglas light-up writing screen, and many other things. Most of the items I had purchased with my own money and was happy to be in a position to give my school possessions to friends.

≫≫≫

THIS IS WHAT MAY LIE AHEAD:

- I will continue to write my daily notes and some poems, but I do not know if I will attempt to write another book. I thought about writing a book about our travels. Joanne and I met a lot of interesting people and saw some strange and unique things in the approximately eighty countries we visited. I have the notes I wrote every day and a photo album for each trip, so I have plenty of good material that would make it an interesting book. I could tell funny stories about the rubes that made asses of themselves. Of course, I would have to be included in that group.

  Joanne and I have a problem remembering peoples' names so we gave nicknames to a lot of the people we met. We'll never forget John-John, Broadway Shmoe, Bossy, Mousy, Burley, Thunder, Smoky, Smarty, Red Wedge, Shutter, and Prattler. When we took a group tour of England, we had nicknames for all thirty seven of the people in our group. A few were Buster Brown, Chipmunk, Pajama Party, Carrot Top, Owl, and T Bone. One lady we met in our group asked us to come to her room because she wanted us to write everyone's pet name on the back of the group picture she purchased. I could go on and on.

  As I mentioned, I have all my daily notes and books of photos so maybe I should write another book about our travels to so many other countries. I think it would be interesting and fun for people to read. I would welcome your advice about this.

- As I get settled into retirement I may want to do more volunteer work. I could volunteer at one of the nearby locations like the Dallas Zoo, Catholic Special Education High School where I attended an open house, or the Dallas aquarium. I could help senior citizens or work with special education and disabled people.

I want to keep active and do some good at the same time. At one point in the past I thought I would like to get an interesting part time job. Some places I have considered are hotels or working the events at the nearby American Airlines Center where professional sports and concerts are held. However, unless things change drastically, currently I do not intend to engage in any type of part time employment. I don't think I would have the time anyway. Since retiring, I have been super busy. The time seems to just fly by. I'm going to keep making the best of my retirement so I don't have a choice but to keep moving forward.

I've heard it said that changes in life can be compared to two planes; one plane lands and at the same time another plane is taking off. I plan to be onboard even if I don't always know where it's headed.

- Joanne and I will have more time to travel. Fortunately, we no longer have to travel in summer when it's hot. Many of the places we like to go can be so crowded.

We plan to see more of the United States. Future travel will of course depend on our health, especially mine. Joanne's health is very good, but mine is kind of iffy. I didn't take care of myself when I was young, however as I've gotten older good health has become more important to me. I've learned a lot and try to follow most of the good health practices that I should at my age.

I do know that Joanne will probably outlive me because she is four years younger than I am, and longevity is common in both her mother's and father's family. Knowing Joanne, after I'm gone she will attract some good and decent man and that will make me happy. Of course, she will never find anyone like me. She likes my personality and outlook, which have been developed over the years from my many life experiences. I think it's good that she won't find someone like me, but I sincerely hope that she occasionally looks back, thinks of me, and smiles. It would be even better if our memories cause her to laugh.

- I know it's a stretch and it may be sometime in the future, but I would like to establish a foundation. Since I know very little about establishing a foundation it might prove to be somewhat complicated. I would like the foundation to be focused on helping special education students and their families. I would name it the Joseph and Leona Anterhaus Foundation. My brother Joe, who was Down syndrome, died twenty nine years ago, and my mom died five years ago. Ideally the foundation would enlist the help of as many volunteers as possible. These people would be former educators or those interested in special education.

CHAPTER 18
FROM COMPOSING POEMS TO WRITING A BOOK

When I was in grade school I had a difficult time in both reading and writing. The only reading material at home I had access to, was the daily newspaper and my comic books. We didn't have a library at school. The public library was only a fifteen minute walk, so I would get books there in the summer months. The turning point for me to becoming a better reader and writer occurred when I entered high school. I always did my homework and tried to do my best in school. Overall, I was fortunate to have very good teachers, such as the nuns from the Sisters of Loretta Order and the various lay women and men. Priests always taught the daily religion classes in my high school.

I got the idea in my late twenties that I wanted to write a book. However, I was working during the day and attending college classes at night, so I did not follow through. When I worked for

Mobil Oil, in my mid-thirties, I wrote a technical manual about how our US Accounting Center could recover from a disaster. I gathered information from each of the seventeen departments, which employed a total of over one thousand people. I worked closely with them to journal the steps necessary to set up procedures for backup. If an event occurred and their departments were totally destroyed, they would use the disaster plan to get back into operation. I documented all my findings in one final book.

It took about a year to do all the work and though it was a good experience, it was not the book I wanted to write. When I was forced to retire from teaching I saw it as a blessing in that it gave me the time and material to fulfill my dream of writing a book. One of the precursors to writing the book was the discipline of writing poems.

Over the years, I have written many poems. Some about various people I encountered along life's journey and especially poems for my sons and the ladies I loved: Anna Marie and Patsye. I'll tell more about her later. Of course, there are the poems I wrote to my one true love, Joanne. I still write to her out of my love, which will endure forever. Then there were some poems which followed a general theme, but were to no one in particular. I spent a good deal of time on the poems, and have always enjoyed the challenge of getting the rhyming words exact to convey my thoughts and feelings.

On the following pages are several of those poems along with my thoughts and feelings when I wrote them. The first two are poems I wrote in the early 1970's. It was a time of conflict in our country. There was a lot of resistance and protests to the Vietnam War. Looking back, my only protesting came in the form of some of my writings. I was a married family man, so I really didn't have the time nor desire to do any formal protesting. I had a day time job, went to school at night, and had a wife and two sons to care for. My wife worked a lot on weekends as a keypunch operator, so I took care of my sons Rob and Keith while she worked. I ran errands, cooked, changed diapers, and when time allowed, watched some football games on television.

FARCE

To market the body for coin

Is to be mocked as a whore

To hawk the soul for materialism

Is an accepted lore

In our refined society some odd doctrines we assume

This is just one reason

Why it is farcical I presume

For example we allow

The wealthy to exploit the poor

As it seems that the affluent

Always need more and more

Satin can emphatically proclaim

The dignified rouge a suitable mate

And both will eventually

Suffer the same fate

When they are removed

To their final tomb

Both will suffer damnation

Of eternal doom

Perhaps a time will come

When injustice will halt abrupt

But only when we realize—

That the system itself is corrupt

MARTYRDOM

The day and night are one
With no fine line of distinction between
At night the stars; at day the sun
The difference not being so keen
But on this I can further expand
Like comparing a beach and a grain of sand
Time will forever be unspent
Right and wrong are not one
It's the difference between a prude and a nude
Because when all is said and done
There is now something definite to conclude
This conclusion is genuine despite being crude
For the corrupt will never stand alone
Wishing only for the opportunity to atone
It's too true that for all their time will come
For the virtuous-
Will suffer MARTYDOM
While the corrupt await idly by—
NUMB

I've always liked to read and usually have four different books going at once. You could say I have a reading addiction. I read biographies, sports books, and history. I've probably read fifteen hundred to two thousand books just on military history. In the past, I mostly read about World War II, but now I am taking the time to read about the Civil War, World War 1, Korea, and Vietnam.

At our home in North Dallas I had a carpenter build wall to wall bookshelves for my collection of books. However, when we moved to our present condo, we just didn't have the room for the books so I put an ad in the newspaper. I sold the collection quickly to a guy who told me he was going to break up the collection and resell the books. I'm sure he made a good profit because there were many rare and first editions.

To feed my addiction to reading, I read the Wall Street Journal, Dallas Morning News, and I subscribe to about twenty five different magazines and newsletters each month. When I come home after being on vacation I read every newspaper, magazine, and newsletter that came while I was gone. I spend thousands of dollars each year on my reading material. It's an expensive and time consuming addiction. Fortunately, I know of no organization that deals with people like me. Perhaps if I had to read using one of those electronic notebooks rather than using paper, I would give up reading. What a horrible thought.

I do not know why I developed such an interest in reading. My grade school and first high school didn't even have libraries. My second high school did have a library, but it was only for use in school. We were not allowed to check a book out to take home. The only reading material we had at our home, except for my school books, were the St. Louis Post Dispatch Newspaper, and my comic books.

The next four poems are a result of my military influence. Being in the military greatly influenced my life in a positive manner. My family benefited in numerous ways when I was active and after I was honorably discharged. Even though initially I didn't want to go into the military, it was one of the best things that ever happened to me. I find it ironic that I never wanted to be a teacher, but through a combination of circumstances and fate became an educator. Another one of the best things that ever happened to me.

LAST WORDS
His wife and son can only inquire why
His best buddy can only attempt to forget
How the young soldier with death did comply
He feared death but his wife and son were his deep regret
On foreign soil he lay dying with no outcry
In a warm pool of blood without a sigh
His whole life he must quickly access
For very soon he knew it would transgress
As the chaplain administer the last sacrament
The young soldier whispered with torment
"Padre, one last request before I die
Write my wife, tell her I love her, and please don't cry
If I could see her and my boy now I'd die content
Tell her I left this world with no regret
Because I feel she has made my life a success
All the happiness she gave me I can't now express
But this is not a time to prophesy
For now the time is near to die
So tell her to do as she must without sentiment
Thank you, Padre; my conscience is now content"

A LONG NIGHT
Gunfire and explosions shatter silence of night
The disciplined grunt takes cover for a firefight
His pleasant thoughts of home are now gone
Even the sweet image of his girl does not linger on
The suffering and death in muffled confusion
For a brief second seem to be a bastard illusion
Then as shrapnel pierces into his flak vest

He grasps war's reality from the pain in his chest
A long night is spent eluding fire and hot steel
Casualties are heavy; it's ugly and sickening real
Finally it over, the enemy has been put to flight
With the sun's first rays of golden light
The young soldier has lived through another night

SAMURAI WARRIOR

To know the taste of absolute victory
The bite of defeat must first be felt
The perfectionist says this can't be
And with him the optimist will agree
Because once defeated the spirit is broken
And the cycle of resistance crestfallen
The fact of the subject is apparent to see
Only when one assumes that man is born free
Initially there's one principal to contradict
Absolute victory can't be assumed to be a solid edit
There never was and never will be
Such a principal as an unrestricted victory
Perhaps the closest thing is to rise above defeat
And to realize defeat is not a reason for shame
There's a fine line between shame and fame
Possibly just enough to know they are not the same
A thousand one hundred forty two years ago
A human being was born in what's now called Asia
His name need not now be mentioned
The unrecorded history of his life is fact enough
Throughout his life he witnessed oppression
His people had been overpowered by people from the north
He spent his life resisting tyranny and injustice

While attempting to plant emotions of resistance within his people

He could accomplish very little change however

Because he could not incite his people to fight

They were peace loving, humble, and meek

A continued existence is all they did persistently seek

A thousand one hundred twenty three years ago

This samurai found what he thought to be absolute victory

As the northerners paraded in force to demoralize his people

He appeared on a small ridge overlooking the field

Seeing the samurai the northerners delayed; they feared a trap

For no one single man could be so self sufficient

They broke columns and formed a rigid defense

Quickly erecting barriers and defensive fortifications

With great composure the samurai observed a ritual

He cleansed his body and offered incense

With care he donned the ceremonial garments for strife

His offering to Buddha for his people would be his life

In his last defiant act he charged the multitude

Within a moment his life was brought to a close

For his people the memory of this moment would be indefinitely froze

The samurai's final gesture to his people was brief

"I can't teach you how to live

So I will suggest to you how to die"

184 years later his people revolted and won their freedom

Can it be that the samurai warrior found absolute victory?

I wrote the next poem, Memorial Day Parade, when my son Rob was going into the military. I was thinking about a Veterans Day

Parade I had recently attended. I don't remember specifically how the parade and Rob's going into the military came together, but I know that some of my deep inner feelings came out in the poem. I named it Memorial Day Parade instead of Veterans' Day Parade, because there is a parade in Dallas on every Veteran's Day, but none that I know of on Memorial Day.

MEMORIAL DAY PARADE

I watched the bands, jeeps, howitzers, and tanks

All four branches of the military marched in precise ranks

As I stood across from the reviewing stand at the Dallas Memorial Day Parade

It came back to me: the adventure, excitement, and a sense of pride

It's something money can't buy: a genuine feeling of pride

It was a pleasant sunny day in which to bask

But not a time to sit by on an aged wine cask

My mind stirred to a time some years ago

When I too proudly wore the military uniform of the US

Thought back to my year of overseas spent in Vietnam

So much of life's joys, cruelties, hopes, and disappointments I saw

Life was adventurous, exciting, novel, and raw

Made a lot of friends I won't ever forget

All we did together: We looked out for each other and cared

Yes indeed it was a special and magical time we shared

While there I traveled to Thailand and Taiwan

Saigon, Vung Tau, Cam Rhan Bay, and Quinon

My base was in Nha Trang on the South China Sea

Surrounded on the other three sides by mountains

It was a privilege in that beautiful country to live among men

Even though there was war, conflict, and stride

I live a relatively happy and as I look back now a simple life

Lived well on about $85.00 a month

The rest of my approximately $400.00 I sent to my family

Because of them I looked forward to a happy future ahead

Now that I'm middle age or what a young person
might call old

I can look back upon a time in my life that was bold

I not only savored and relished it

But I learned a lot about how life is offhandedly cast

That it's challenging, fragile, and goes too fast

Robbie your military career is now very near and I'm glad

But of course your going away leaves me rather sad

I guess I must accept that, it's something I can't
and shouldn't control

But let it be so that no matter how far apart

We remain bonded within the spirit of the heart

Let me give you a few word of advice

Fully enjoy your life; you'll only live it once not twice

Think positive and make the most of everything you do

No matter what happens always look at the good side

Steer the turns of joy, hope, and happiness extremely wide

This has been difficult for me to write

You're a grown man and I must now see that fact in an
existing light

I wish I were venturing with you but that not to be

Then again maybe in a way I am going along too

No matter where or how far you go I'll be in part with you!

Make "Good Luck" always be your companion, Robbie.

I wrote the next poem in November of 1979. The period from 1970
to 1978 was really hard for me. There were the issues with my job
at Mobil Oil, I was attending college to get both my degree from
SMU and then my Master's Degree from the University of Dallas,
and my wife and I were experiencing problems in our marriage.

As stated earlier in the book, Anna Marie left in May of 1978,
and we were divorced by October. I received custody of my sons,
Robbie and Keith, and we stayed in our house on Partridge Lane
in Irving, Texas. She took the boys every other weekend, and we
made arrangements for holidays and when she wanted to take
them on vacation. A few years later, I paid Anna Marie for her
share of the house.

Over time the initial shock wore off and I realized that as a
result of our divorce both Anna Marie and I were better off. I also
realized that our divorce had a very adverse and devastating effect
on our sons. It affected them at the time when they were so young,
but even more so later in life. When we divorced, Rob was twelve
years old and Keith was ten. I am truly sorry and will always regret
the consequences they experienced resulting from our divorce. I
will have to live with that regret for the rest of my life.

Suddenly, I was caring for the boys, the house, and for the first
time dating other girls. I never dated anyone other than Anna
Marie before. The nuns would say I was a good Catholic boy. Many

others, including myself, would say I was a dumb Catholic boy. I slowly started to smarten up about girls at the age of thirty four. I guess as the saying goes "better late than never."

I didn't get off to a real good start because my first date didn't show up. I met her at the Mountain People Ski Club that I had joined. The Club went on snow skiing trips, canoe trips, and backpacking trips. Once a month, they held a happy hour at a local club. I met a girl at the first party I attended and arranged a date for us to go water skiing the following weekend. I asked my friend Mark and his girlfriend to join us. That Saturday morning I went to get gas in the boat and when I returned home, my son told me she had called and cancelled. So my first date ended up being me, my son Keith, my friend Mark, and his girlfriend. We actually had a good time and I soon forgot the girl's name.

Dating was a slow learning process for me and I am proud to say I was always the gentleman. I didn't have much money, but I had a good sense of humor. I was in my mid-thirties, so I focused my dating efforts on younger ladies. Interestingly, most of them didn't cook, but relished coming to my house for a home cooked meal. Of course, being a pretty good cook, I never let them down.

Then I finally met Joanne, who was a little younger than me, and was an excellent cook. We enjoyed numerous dinners at her home and mine and took great pleasure in the cooking and cleaning. Today, we still do and don't particularly like going out to dinner because our home cooking is much better. However, we do enjoy going to restaurants in other countries, so we can try different foods and cook them at home. We also visit the grocery stores to find spices or dried foods to bring home so we can experiment using them in our own creative dishes. I hit the jackpot with Joanne!

I wrote several poems over a few years after my first wife and I divorced. My life was spinning in a helter-skelter spiral and writing helped me to keep a sense of logic.

ACTS OF COURAGE

What exactly is courage?
Can you give me an answer that's exact?
Or just give me an example that's a true fact
While you're thinking it over,
I'll go ahead and tell you my thoughts
Too often it's associated with an act of war
But there's no need to look that far
Courage is far more common;
It's doing what one thinks is right
Even though there's going to be one hell of a fight.
It's standing up to something that's wrong
When things go bad to still feel the pulse of a song
It's having the discipline to do as you feel
To always be yourself; to be real
It's getting out of bed when you can't face another day
And having the fortitude to do as you feel and to do as you say
It's leading a life that's dull and somewhat mild
Because you're doing your best to raise a child
Now let me explain briefly what courage isn't
It's not a total absence of fear
For as a general rule
This is the mark of a fool
We've all got to face some strife
One last thought-
Courage can't be bought.

The next poem I wrote to my son Rob in April of 1980. He was in his last year of middle school. There was a boy he knew who attended high school who threatened him. Several carloads of friends showed up at Rob's school so they could watch the boy beat up Rob. I had no idea what had happened until our phone started ringing off the hook later that evening. Apparently, Rob got the best of the boy in a fist fight. Rob's friends reported that the high school boy ended up crying in his car in the arms of his girlfriend.

STREET FIGHTER

The street fighter is well versed in alley fighting
He's fast as a bolt of West Texas lightening
Sometimes a person has no choice
As to whether he wants to fight or not
It's easier to give than to take a hard shot
When you're forced to fight
And you're sure you're in the right
Be as brilliant as the first morning light
It's not a time to be shy
You'd best bust open a nose or an eye
Sometimes your feet feel like lead
It smarts to take a hard shot in the head
During a fight there's not much to be said
Again, fight only for a good reason
But definitely fight hard
Think, be swift, and keep up your guard
Remember even an ace is beaten by a wild card
If you fight for what's right it's no hunch
You'll always be the one to have the last punch
When it's over retain an inner compassion

The bible says every man is your brother
Remember Robbie—
We're all street fighters in one way or another

The next two poems go together. The first titled "Happy Father's Day" was written by my son Rob, who was fourteen years old at the time, and given to me on Father's Day in 1980. The second poem was my response to him aptly titled "Response to Robbie."

HAPPY FATHER'S DAY

It seems like you have done quite a lot for me,
That's why I'm writing this poem you see.
I know all the things that you've gone through
Maybe that's another reason I write this poem to you
I speak of the divorce you know,
And maybe a couple problems you sometimes show.
I'll always know you're the best father by far,
And I hope when I get older I'm the kind you are.
I will always try to make you proud.
This poem may not have much talent or length,
But I let it express my feelings for your strength.
There are a few more words to make this poem complete.
They are I love you, Happy Father's Day, and thank you
For teaching me to walk on my own two feet.

RESPONSE TO ROBBIE

Robbie, I like the poem you wrote for me
I'll keep it if I live to be a hundred and three
It will confirm my belief that the best in life is free
You said maybe it didn't have much talent or length
But I can assure you that it is extremely talented

Length of just about anything isn't relevant in the end
For as a general rule, the longer something is, the sooner it
will bend
What counts in writing or in a person is what's inside
Your scope of thought is extremely wide
Let me now add a few other thoughts of my own
I say them not with the air of vanity
Although I realize that words can effect eternity
Because the influence and result of them may never stop
Words of true wisdom are the most valuable gift I know
For they help you to mentally and spiritually grow
You know I can see some of myself in you
So what I tell you I honestly perceive to be true
Men who stand out by themselves are few
I think every man should live out his dream
No matter how strange or far out of line it may seem
Always remember exactly who you are
Evaluate where and how you went; not just how far
Life can't be lived in a vacuum jar
So don't ever be afraid to stand alone
Because when everything is over and done
You'll know within that you will have thoroughly won
You'll be able to live with yourself
So I suggest you conform to your own standards
Remain proud as you be and stay your own person
And have the courage and strength among men to stand out
You'll find that's what life is really about
I hope these words don't sound too complex or involved
But only too soon you'll be on your own
You will go far; Have a family and your own home
I hope you'll have a son or daughter who will write you a poem

I wrote the next poem, "The Outcast," in the 1970's. I do not remember why I wrote it. I didn't care much for desk jobs so I would get away from the desk as much as possible. Maybe my feelings of discontent somehow contributed to the poem about the unnamed character in my poem. He is labeled an outcast by others, but he is quite content with his life. Personally, up to that point I could be labeled a success by some, but my life was far from content. I think you will concur that many people considered successful are actually discontent. No matter how you cut it, life can be tough. There is an anonymous quote with which I fully agree, "Life is the only thing you can't get out of alive."

THE OUTCAST

He lived on a darkened bayou quite remote
In a one room dilapidated shed
He owned a small wooden boat
And a bible which he seldom read
He claimed a book couldn't teach reverence
It was more important how a man's life was led
At twilight one evening while we fished
The old man cracked a beer and casually said
"Son, I tend to treat life with indifference
At times like I don't have a lick of sense in my head
Oh yea I've heard a few say I'm an outcast
And that from life's reality I have fled
This is true, at least to some extent
But here I feel there is a contrast
Briefly look at the other side of the coin instead
In this place there is a void of violence
It's calm. It's peaceful. It's vast
The plants and animals are a constant magnificence

Even when the sky is dark and overcast
It projects an inner feeling of benevolence
It's not important that I'm labeled an outcast
Because it's not I who am grossly misled
The swamp is such a tranquil place for repose
Who can say that I should transpose
I live my life as only I have choose"

"The Stripper," my next poem, was written in either 1969 or 1970.
My friend John Wayne Payne (his real name) and I worked for
the Texas Pacific Railroad and attended night classes together
for two years. Our classes were held on Monday nights at SMU's
downtown campus. There was a strip club named, "The Busy Bee,"
located on Industrial Blvd., which was not too far away. So we
would often frequent the Busy Bee before attending our 7:00 P.M.
class. In those days, the ladies were never fully nude, but wore
G-strings and used pasties to cover a portion of their breasts. We
found the club an excellent way to prepare for class by shaking off
the dust from a long day working our rail transportation jobs.

THE STRIPPER
The rigid jawbone of a stubborn ass
The firm ass of a commercialized woman
Who for now I'll just call Shady Katy
Her body's lean and mean
With a mind that's not too keen
But in a dull light she could pass for a beauty queen
She works happy hour until close up as a stripper
Moving gracefully as a cat with a soft purr
She teasingly removes her silver fur
Shady Katy loves them all
Loves 'em big and loves them small

A long time ago she really loved a dude
But dumped him when she was in the mood
What happens when she's finished at thirty years old?
They'll turn her out in the cold
Just telling her she has a commodity that can still be sold
There's no old folks home for a has been stripper
Not even a Gypsy Rose Lee Hall of Fame
I'm not attempting to cut her down or place any blame
I only want to make this point-
Inner and outer beauty, just aren't the same.

In 1970 while working at the Texas Pacific Railway, Fred who was a fellow coworker and good friend, died. He was in his early sixties but had suffered from severe medical problems for years. Prior to his death he was struggling with crippling arthritis and had difficulty walking.

When I found out Fred had died, I visited the funeral home to pay my respects. I arrived about 6:30 p.m. and stayed for quite a while. No one else was present, it was just Fred, me, and my memories. So I penned, "A Friend Departs" as a tribute to him.

When I worked with him he was a simple file clerk, but as a young man he had held a high profile sales solicitor position in Pittsburg, Pennsylvania. I never knew why he had been demoted from such a high profile position. More than a few occasions Fred had told me that as a young man he quaffed his share of drinks and enjoyed numerous female companions. So, I along with everyone else assumed his active lifestyle had caused problems and demoting him was the railroad's way of instilling discipline while saving his career.

Everyone at the office liked Fred and admired his spunk in dealing with his disabilities. Occasionally, several of us would frequent a bar on Akard Street and have a few beers after work. I haven't thought of Fred for years, but he was a good friend. Today, before writing this piece I passed by the parking lot, where the bar once stood, on my way to the YMCA. I still remembered all the good times Fred and the rest of us had. I think I will drink a beer or two in his memory.

A FRIEND DEPARTS

His family wasn't at the wake
He made more than just one mistake
I didn't know him in a family sense
I was there only because he was my friend
Of life's physical pleasures he did partake
Not caring that his life was opaque
Possibly it was in reality poetic justice
That there was no grief at his wake
Sorrow shouldn't be only for its own sake
I never made it a point to judge
Nor to care if his soul was slightly tarnished
or congealed black
There's no need to fabricate words that are fake
But really for me it was easy to comprehend
I paid my respects to say adios to my friend

"Open House" is a poem I wrote that Joanne and I included on the invitation to our wedding reception that was to be held on July 15, 1984. We invited our friends, neighbors, coworkers, my former wife Anna Marie, Joanne's former husband Rich, and some of Rich's relatives. We wanted everyone to know our marriage was going to be good for everyone. My former wife decided not to come, but Rich attended along with a date. Rich's brother and his wife also came. Many people attended and it was a happy and great day we will never forget. However, it was also somewhat of a sad day. Joe, my brother who was Down syndrome, died suddenly at age twenty seven, just two days before our wedding day. I went to his funeral in St. Louis, Missouri the day after our reception.

OPEN HOUSE

Joanne and Bob are being married July 14

There will be an open house the next day

Come and be our guest

And share in our wedding fest

It's a very special occasion for us

But we prefer it casual dress with no fuss

So instead of bringing a package or gift

Just bring your photograph we can keep

Feelings of happiness and togetherness are much more deep

There will be wine, food, and sparking water

You'll meet our three sons and pretty daughter

The date is Sunday, July 15

Open house from 3 to 7

At 3817 Alta Vista in Dallas

We'd like you to be our guest

Nothing better could we request

When I sat down to write a book based on my experiences during my teaching career, military service, and life in general, my goal was that it would be interesting reading and stir some debate about the various trials facing our country.

My wife occasionally tells me I am obnoxious. Then she quickly reminds me she is only joking. Upon reading the content of the book I will leave it to you, the reader, to either agree or disagree with her. Of course, you are free to add whatever colorful adjectives that might lend credence to her description of me.

It is my hope that you will agree with my comparisons of the DISD and the state of our military during the Vietnam War. However, I'd like to point out that what I wrote is only what I saw. There is always the bigger picture one must take into account. My expressions are a mere peek into the overall picture, like peering through the knothole in a fence at a parade. I saw a portion of the parade as it passed my line of sight. Thankfully, the events of my life led me toward a career in teaching. Thus the reason the story line expressed in the book are at times sporadic and extensive. On the previous pages and the pages to come I have stated true facts along with my personal assessment, beliefs, and opinions.

CHAPTER 19
LAST THOUGHTS FOR NOW

When I was young, I was a deep thinker and recorded many of my thoughts, opinions, and concerns. I think in some ways this had a negative effect on me because a lot of things occurring in my life were beyond my control. As I got older, I still wrote my daily journal notes and poems, but I took life's events less seriously. This new freedom helped me to maintain more of a balanced attitude and to accept whatever happened that was beyond my control.

I was at a party many years ago and sharing some of my deep thoughts with my friend's wife. She said I must be an Aquarius. She explained how she knew this because of my outlook and feelings. I forget the details now of what she said. She was correct in that I am an Aquarius. I do not follow or know much about Zodiac characteristics, but I remember it well even after many years. It may or may not have some relevancy. I hope I didn't get on her nerves too much that night. Sometimes, I guess I could be annoying when

I rambled on about some tangent or two, especially after having a few beers. Now when I have a few too many cervezas, I do just the opposite and get much calmer. I think that's good because I conserve what energy I have for more important activities or maybe it's because I am older and don't have an overabundance of vigor.

I kept many of my own thoughts and some things that I read over the years that I considered relevant. I wrote these in a separate notebook which I referred to many times. I remember why I wrote some of these statements, but do not remember others because they were written over a period of years. I still have my notebook, so I will use it to condense some of these reflections to pass on to you for your consideration. Let me begin with a list of things that were important to my success as a special education teacher.

1. **Do not hesitate to make friends but know who your true friends are and continue to cultivate the growth of those friendships.**

    I think in general it's easier for young people especially children and teenagers to quickly make new friends. I'll give you an example from my own life. During my first day as a freshman at Blessed Sacrament High School in my homeroom class, I sat in a desk right behind Jerry Rose. He was the first person I met, and we formed a quick friendship, which lasted until he died at age fifty five of Multiple Sclerosis. Jerry lived in Father Dunn's Catholic Home for Boys in St. Louis, but when he graduated from high school, he moved to live with his aunt and uncle who lived just two blocks from my parents' house. We even joined the Air Force together. He was responsible for my meeting Anna Marie Monaco, whom I latter married, so my friendship with Jerry greatly affected my life in many ways.

As we grow older, some people can still make friends rapidly, but it becomes harder for others. I think some of us tend to drift away from the friends we have. Life moves at a fast pace, but it's important to maintain our friendships. With the telephone, Email, and texting, it's fairly easy to keep in touch, but we must take the initial step to do so.

2. **Be aware of your achievements and reward yourself in an appropriate manner.**

You need to be able to forgive yourself for any wrongs, misdeeds, or numskull actions. I think most people tend to judge themselves too harshly. I know I did when I was young. The trick is to think positive in general and to stress your positive points rather than dwelling on negative elements. Viewing others in this manner completes a positive cycle and can lead to win-win situations. It could be a hard habit for some to get into, but it is well worth the effort. Being a teacher is so complicated and fast paced that making some mistakes is a given.

I remember that I explained my concept of self-judgment to a teacher friend by using Ted Williams, the famous baseball player, as an example. He is famous for hitting 406 in 1941. This basically means for every 10 times Ted Williams batted he got 4 hits and made 6 outs. Ted Williams is considered one of the best hitters in baseball history. So let's go easy on ourselves when we strike out once in a while.

3. **Have pride in yourself but maintain a sense of humor.**

I think that maintaining a positive attitude helps people to feel good and to maintain feelings of pride. Guys listen up. I've read in several places that the one thing that attracts ladies to certain men is the guys' sense of humor. Let's expand on that and apply humor to personal, business, and regular daily living situations when it's appropriate. I think a little humor can go a long way to adding a little zest to life. Humor is especially important to any teacher, but I think even to a greater degree for a Special Education teacher. I always enjoyed talking and sharing stories with other teachers. Some of the narrations were hilarious, but they surely weren't funny when they occurred.

4. **Fortune favors the bold.**

When the people who are bold take some drastic action, it's usually a complete success or a total failure. In view of this, it's best to get as much information as possible before initiating any activity. It might be possible to learn a lot by contacting other people, observing similar situations, or analyzing available information.

From my experience, it's mainly best to do something rather than nothing when a decision is at hand. But at the same time, I've found that using all available time to think things through is usually better than making a "quick draw" decision.

5. **Live fully in the present but plan for the future.**

I've heard it said that yesterday is gone, tomorrow may not be, and you only have today to live. In my opinion, the statement is true only to a certain extent.

I agree that it's not good to dwell on the past or excessively spending time worrying about the future. However, I think remembering the past is important because we should remember past mistakes so they won't be repeated. We should remember good events and people from the past because it lifts our spirits and helps to maintain positive passions. I believe planning for the future is very important because what we do today will affect what happens in the future. Maintaining a proper balance is the key, and the present is the most important.

I told my fellow members at the Mobil Oil Pegasus Toastmasters Club when I left Mobil. "Challenge yourselves. Times may be good or times may be bad, but they're the only times you have."

6. Observe and ask questions.

Both my sister Linda and my wife Joanne ask people so many questions that I tell them they should be detectives. Of course they ask many questions because they are good at observing and want to know more. I think most people appreciate that both of them are interested in them and do not mind answering the questions.

I am guilty of not being a skillful observer in general, but when I was a teacher I tried to have a 360 degree vision. I needed to maintain that perception in order to assure success and to avoid mishaps or calamities. I also did not hesitate to ask questions of other staff members or administrators.

I found it especially helpful to ask questions when I was at numerous teacher workshops and met teachers from other schools who I did not know. While we were sitting at the same table waiting or doing some of the many group activities, I would ask questions about their school, class, activities, methods of doing documentation, or numerous other things. I could also tell them of my activities, and we could make beneficial comparisons.

I know I will never be the interrogator Linda and Joanne are, but now that I'm retired I can take it easier because I can rely on the two ladies to see, ask questions, and then tell me what they discovered.

7. **Realize life is short but be patient and don't rush.**

As we get older, time seems to go faster. I know when I was young school time seemed to drag by. I thought I can't wait to become an adult so I could do whatever I want to do. When I became an adult, I found out that life doesn't work that way and in many ways life is even more challenging.

I think I wrote the statement about being patient and don't rush when I had a job at Mobil that I really despised. I even interviewed at other places to find another job. I found a very good job at the Army and Military Exchange Headquarters in Dallas. The problem was that the job was in Staten Island, New York. I was married with two children and was about half way through the courses to get my Master's Degree. I thought about the opportunity seriously, but I did not take the job. Instead I stayed at my job that I detested. Within a year, I got a promotion to a job in the same department that I really liked, and I even got my own office. I forced myself to be as patient as I could, and over the years it has paid off.

I guess the moral to this story is that even a blind hog will find some acorns if it's patient enough to keep trying.

8. **Meet new people and be willing to learn from them and when appropriate utilize their talents.**

We previously talked about making new friends, but let's take this a step further and discuss simply working with others in a coordinated effort to achieve success. When we work together and utilize each other's talents we all benefit personally in some way. Of course, I've known many throughout my teaching and business career who helped others simply because they wanted to and expected no immediate reward.

The teaching profession should be similar to a large family environment where each member is ready to help each other. The veterans or more experienced teachers should be prepared to help the newer teachers.

9. **People's names are important to them, so try to remember their names or nicknames. It's OK to give them a nickname but tread carefully and be sure they like the new christening.**

I think most will agree with this suggestion. I remember spending an evening in the Dale Carnegie Course working on methods how to remember a person's name. The course helped me because before I could remember faces from many years in the past, but I forgot names quickly.

I've noticed how regular education teachers learn their students' names so quickly at the beginning of the year. Some use name tags they put on the students' desks for the first week of school.

I'm going to tell you an unbelievable story about my sister Linda's name. She was born when I was about ten years old. I remember when she was a little girl my mom would call her Linda Lee. Everyone else just called her Linda. When my sister went to get her Missouri's driver license, she found out her legal name was Leona Linda. Visibly and justifiably upset, she asked our mom about her real name and was told my dad wanted her first name to be Leona which was my mom's first name. How in the world could she have gone through seventeen years of her life not knowing her real name?

I know that times were sure different in the 1950's and 60's, especially where we lived, so I can see why she didn't find out her real name at school. I don't know why my parents didn't tell her the correct name. I guess like most families, ours had its strange schemes. Thus it appears to be a far-fetched tale, but it's true-blue and is an extreme example about the importance of a person's name.

10. Think positive and believe in achieving success.

Having an open mind and thinking things through is important for success. I don't think it's good to be overly positive, but avoiding a defeatist attitude is a must. A person should also be ready to allow the time required for success to come about.

A good example of was the twelve years I took to get my four year Bachelor's degree. I attended evening college courses and even took correspondence courses when I was in Vietnam. There were some obstacles to overcome, but I always felt that I would get my college degree.

For instance when I was stationed at Mather AFB, I attended Sacramento City College two evenings a week. There was one course that required an expensive book. Anna Marie and I were living on only a few hundred dollars a month, so I borrowed the book from the base library and renewed it every three weeks for the whole semester.

After taking so long to get my bachelor's degree, I got my master's degree in the next two and a half years. Without a degree, I would not have got my job at Mobil Oil and of course could not have been a teacher. I once quit high school, but even though it took me twelve years I never quit college. Granted, I did have some unplanned detours in obtaining my degree, but my stubbornness and dogged determination paid off.

11. **Keep up with current events.**

Some people like to watch the world news or read the Metro Section of the newspaper to find out what is happening in the world or in the local area. I do this to a large extent too. Sometimes what affects us even more is what is happening at our jobs, in our neighborhood, or with our friends and relatives. It's easy to overlook what is so close to us. I know I tended to overlook the obvious when I was in the business world, which definitely did not help my career.

In most cases, what is occurring around us in our daily lives will affect us much more than something that is happening on the other side of the country or world.

12. **Accept or ignore criticism while not wasting time or effort to criticize.**

When I took the Dale Carnegie Course, our instructors taught us to never criticize, condemn, or complain. In our society, that advice is hard to follow for most of us. After reading this book, many of you may be thinking I need to retake the Carnegie Course. That could be true, so I better change the topic away from myself and talk about a common characteristic I've seen among many principals.

The principals I had were positive and tried to approach others in a confident manner. What I have especially noted is that they did not argue issues that are irrelevant or that might get heated or out of control. I've learned from them that it's sometimes best to say nothing or to keep things in order by moving ahead in another realistic direction.

13. Learn a lesson from each good or bad experience.

It's natural to overly remember our good experiences and to forget the bad ones. I've found that writing a daily journal forces me to reflect on what happened in order to write it down. Since I have kept a journal for the last 39 years, I can read my notes and comprehend events that occurred in the past in a clear manner.

Some of the things that I don't even remember from years past can be important in understanding either good or bad overall experiences. To use an analogy, it's like taking the many pieces of a puzzle. The pieces themselves show little, but when the puzzle is put together it reveals a full and clear picture.

14. Hard times will bring out the best or the worst in people.

My personal opinion is that tough times in most people's lives will rally them to do the best they can under the circumstance to try to move ahead. I witnessed this several times in my life.

My first wife left after we were married thirteen years. Looking back a lot of people, even my relatives in Missouri, seemed to know she was going to leave. I had no idea and was the last one to find out. I was devastated, but fortunately I was very busy taking care of the boys, shopping for groceries, cooking, and washing our clothes. In fact, I didn't even know how to operate the washer and dryer before she left.

Yes, I believe tough times will either bring out the highest degree of good or abominable characteristics in a person. Fortunately, I had the boys to help bring out one of the highest endeavors in my life. I realize, and I'm sure the boys know, I made a lot of mistakes, but I think we all understand that I always did the best I could at the time.

In the 1970's it was very rare for a man to get custody of their children but Anna Marie agreed to my taking the kids and her having liberal visitation with them. Whenever I went to Missouri, I made sure to take the boys to Anna Marie's parents and her relatives' houses. Even when I went by myself, I would sometimes visit them and her whole family was always gracious and nice to me.

I've told several people over the years that I was a lucky guy to have two such magnificent mothers-in-law. Both Anna Marie's and Joanne's mothers were both the best I could ever hope for.

15. Anything can be lost so enjoy all of your present daily life

First of all, I think it's important to enjoy what you have. It's easy to take things for granted. For example, when I had my job at Mobil Oil I seldom stopped to think how good I had it in so many ways, but once I left I was devastated. I did just the opposite during my teaching career. I enjoyed every day in some way or another and most days I fully enjoyed the whole day.

I finally learned to "stop and smell the roses." Of course that's easier to do in a job you love rather than just tolerate. One of the most important things I tell young people is to do something in life you enjoy and want to do. I myself was just lucky that Mobil let me go, and I became a teacher. I didn't plan it that way, but I'm so pleased that after my life fell apart, there emerged a "heavenly phoenix" that morphed me into a Special Education Teacher.

The key point to keep in mind is to relax in order to appreciate and relish what you have. Even the small things in life should be noted and enjoyed. One never knows when they will lose a job, loved one, or good health. Pick up any daily newspaper and there will be many heartbreaking examples of sudden events that drastically affect various people, which in turn touch their friends, relatives, and other peoples' lives.

Remember no one owes you anything and everyone has his or her own problems. Life had many challenges for everyone both rich and poor. Just reading a daily newspaper will usually prove this statement. Many feel that a parent, son, daughter, or other relative is obligated to take care of them. When they do help, it's frequently not enough for the needy rascal. When I wrote this statement, I was in my mid-thirties. Up to that point in my life no one helped me financially or materially, but a few sure helped me in a moral nature. In my opinion the moral help was of more value than any material help.

 I told you earlier how Sister Cornelia helped me when I quit high school. By getting me a part time job so I could graduate she helped me to help myself. Her method turned out to be much more valuable throughout my life than if she had been in a position to give to me financially.

Another example is when Uncle Sam took me as a backward doltish teenager and taught me to be an alert man of the world during my three years six months of military service. I can never properly repay Sister Cornelia or Uncle Sam for all they did for me, but I realize I owe them a mountain of gratitude. So for now I'll just say, "Thank you both from the bottom of my heart."

\\\

I have another section in my notebook where I wrote things that are important to avoid doing. I wish I could say that I adhered to my own directives throughout my adult life, but when I was young I violated many of my written statements. As I got older and calmed down to some extent, I did better. In some ways, I think it is harder to avoid doing the wrong things than it is to just do the right things. The ideal situation is when a people person can adhere to the majority of their personal do and no do lists. First they must first have some system to set goals. The system can be formal, such as when I write out my goals or informal when they are known to a person in some other way. Here is my list of no-nos.

1. **Don't give up hope or say, "It can't be done."**

It's human nature to be in a depressed mood when things go wrong. When they things are going awry, it can be like an avalanche tumbling down a mountain. When detrimental events occur they can go from bad to worse quickly. Judging from the various disasters that occurred in my life, I've found that just doing my best during the crisis helps to keep my head above water until time comes to the rescue. Avoiding a complete negative outlook is important. A person does not have to have a "Pollyanna" outlook, thinking all is going to go from bad to perfect. To think that way is neither practical nor likely to happen.

For instance I was let go at General Portland Cement Company, which at the time came as a complete surprise to me. As a matter of fact my wife Anna Marie was going to the bank that day to pay off $1,000 we owed on our 69 Pontiac. We didn't have much more than that, so right after I found out I telephoned the bank. She was getting ready to make the payment. When they put her on the telephone I told her the bad news, and she burst out crying right in the middle of the bank.

Back then there was no lay off compensation like there is now. I was told I had a month to work, but could leave during the day if I had a job interview. Each day I went somewhere to interview for a job and it was frustrating to get the "cold shoulder" at each place. The worst experience I had was at Bra-niff Airline Headquarters. They more or less told me in some-what of a rude manner, "Don't let the door hit you on the way out, Jack." During the third week, I interviewed at both Bell Helicopter and Mobil Oil. I got job offers from both. I was lean-ing toward the Bell Helicopter job because it involved work-ing full speed making choppers for countries around the world including many for the Shah of Iran and for our military forces in Vietnam. I decided to take the Mobil job because my evening courses at SMU were in downtown Dallas, and the Bell job was located miles away between Dallas and Fort Worth. Mobil also made an exception when hiring me. Mobil required a college degree to get the job and I was within one fall semester from graduating.

As it turned out Mobil was a much better choice because of their benefits and location, Of course helicopter sales dropped off after the Vietnam War, and the Shah of Iran was over-thrown. I know I keep saying this, but I think it's true that the Good Lord was looking out for me.

2. Don't downgrade yourself or think negative.

I think a lot or even most people at times think of their own lives in a very negative manner. One proof of this is the many suicides around the world, especially the suicides of teenagers or young people. I believe that as our society has become much more complicated it puts more pressure on everyone. Yes, we benefit from our modern conveniences and technology, but there is a price to be paid.

For example, when I was a boy we had no personal com-puters or no Internet. I've read over the last several years how some social sites on the Internet have played a part in ruining people's lives or even resulted in some suicides. Some might say that there are millions using social sites, and the percentage of these negative events is extremely low. Maybe the percentage occurrences are low to the overall number of users, but our very complex society contributes to self-depreciation in hundreds of other ways, but it's the society we live in, and we can't undo progress.

In order to avoid negative thinking, it's important to keep active and to accomplish some positive events whenever we can. I was fortunate in my teaching career to experience positive events every day. Of course I had some bad days over the years as a teacher, but I'll guarantee you that they were microscopic compared to the number of up-hill days I incurred in the business world.

When I worked At Mobil Oil, I started jogging in the morning before work because it made me feel better and helped me make it through the day. I would drive to McArthur High School in Irving, Texas, and run six miles around the track. I had to get up at 4:00 a.m. and I ran two, three, or four days a week. I was addicted to running much as some people get habituated to nicotine or alcohol. After I started teaching, I was able to quit running because I would go to the spa to exercise, swim, and use the steam room or sauna before work a few days a week.

3. Don't over compare people or situations.

It's a natural instinct to compare just about anything and everything. For example, when we go to the grocery store to buy meat or fruit, we compare them to the other fruits or pieces of meat and try to purchase the best quality for the best price.

I think it's good to make some comparisons, but I don't think this should be the only reason to make a decision. For example, many people, especially young ones, make decisions on dating and even marriage proposals based on their physical attraction of a person. Especially when they are comparing someone with above average looks to the majority of other candidates with just average looks.

This reminds me what I learned in a noncredit class I took at North Lake College in Irving. It was not long after I was divorced and the class dealt with new divorcees adjusting to single life. The class consisted of five women, our female instructor, and me. During the first class, we each told about ourselves. I don't remember a lot about what several of the women said or even myself for that matter. But, I specifically remember what one fairly attractive lady said. "I want to meet a decent man. I don't care if he's bald and fat as long as he's good to me and my kids." Well, I wasn't bald and fat at that time in my life so I knew I better not ask her for a date. Of course, I was nowhere near ready for another relationship at that time.

〜〜〜

I have a section in my notebook labeled Philosophy, which come from something I read or have noted in various places. Other statements I thought of myself. I will discuss some of these statements. The last one about Masada is somewhat off base, but I think it relates to this book because it stirs and conveys deep passions of the human spirit.

〜〜〜

1. **My friend J D Lovelace at Mobil oil, who was a World War II veteran, told me this about happiness, "It is having someone to love, something to look forward to, and something to do."**

   He also told me, several of the older men in Texas with the most wisdom, were named with just two initials or went throughout life being called by just two initials. He mentioned two, G W and R Q, who were also World War II veterans. He said these good ol' Texas boys were laid back and fairly deep thinkers. I think J D was right in what he said. He only told me this once, but I never forgot it.

   I remember one evening J D, my brother in law, another man from Mobil and his young son, and I went fishing in my boat on Lake Ray Hubbard near Dallas. We fished until late that night using a lantern which we hung over the side of the boat to attract fish. The boy caught one fish, and no one else caught anything. The lad was happy, because it was the first fish he ever caught, plus he showed the adults up by snagging a fish. The rest of us were just happy to be out at night fishing.

2. **Various societies define values differently.**

   When I made this notation in my journal it was many years ago and I was referring to different nations, cultures, and religions. As I think about my entry now, I would include people of different religions, races, wealth, countries, and even neighborhoods or areas of the same country.

   I recently visited India and our tour guide told me that at least 80 percent of their marriages were still arranged by the families. The couple had to be in the same caste, and if the couple was Hindu the horoscope must be good for both families. I can see how this arrangement could have advantages and disadvantages, but in our country most non-Indians would never even consider an arranged marriage.

I asked our guide how the divorce rate in India compared to the rate in the USA. He answered that it was much lower in India.

A less complex example involves the use of a term of expression which held different meanings in different areas of the country. When I was at Mobil Oil, my friend Lance saw a well-dressed woman in the company cafeteria. He asked her if she was "slumming it." It seemed where he came from in Illinois the expression meant relaxing or taking it easy. Later the woman asked me why my friend had accused her of being in a slum because she was eating in the company cafeteria. I just told her, "Lance is a cold dude." My statement probably confused her even more, but it got Lance off the hook for a while.

3. Make your own decisions based on true needs.

Often our decisions are based on what is expected of us, input from others, or determinations without much thought involved. We all make most decisions on what we want and need, but what we desire is not always what we require. I find younger people often make decisions out of what they desire not giving much thought to what might be required.

Life moves at a fast pace, so there's not always a lot of time to think of all aspects of our decisions. All of us are going to make wrong decisions so the important thing is to learn from them and use that information for future events. As I previously said, my wife and I have been to about eighty countries. Each time we go on one of our trips, we continue to make mistakes. We try to learn from them and not make the same mistake twice. We continue to learn from our blunders. We have found that traveling to other countries and observing their cultures is one of life's best learning experiences.

Some of our friends and relatives wonder why we spend so much money on our travels. That's a story in itself, but throughout the years of our marriage, we've had a part time business to make money to support our travel addiction.

We have bought and sold various items such as antiques, military items, jewelry, old toys, ladies designer clothes, sports memorabilia, or anything else we could make a buck on. We would pay for one to three tables and show our goods at weekend gun shows, antique shows, toy shows, flea markets, or similar venues. It was a lot of work to get ready for the shows, to set up, to spend the time there, to break down our exhibits, and to come home and put everything away. However, we met many interesting people and enjoyed the buying, trading, and selling.

We also made good money over the years buying and selling sets of golf clubs. We'd buy golf clubs at garage sales, flea markets, and through ads in the thrift newspapers. When we accumulated several sets we'd put an ad in the newspaper. Over the years we sold hundreds of sets of golf clubs. I always told Joanne that we saved many marriages because the men would play golf instead of going to bars and strip clubs.

Trust me I know those environments are not healthy because I frequented those places when I was a young man. Fortunately, I got them out of my system many years ago, so now my addiction is staying home with Joanne where we enjoy cooking, watching reality TV shows, and venturing out on our various adventures.

It is good that I made an ass of myself early in my life and no longer exhibit those behaviors because there is an old expression, "There's no fool like an old fool."

4. **Look upon everything as temporary and nothing as permanent.**

Everything changes over time. The only exception to this may be the statement that "true love lasts forever." I look at the newspaper obituaries every day which I can't help reading. When I read through them I see two things that I always notice. I see how some couples have been married for fifty, sixty, or even seventy years. I see that true love existed between them and that it does indeed last forever. I also notice the age of the people who passed away, especially when they are younger than I am.

Some might say that the obituary section of the newspaper is morbid, but I disagree with them. I point out to them that the information about the peoples' lives and the pictures of the deceased can be real "eye openers."

5. **Don't ever give up.**

Masada's baron mountain towers above the Dead Sea like the fortress it once was after the destruction of Jerusalem in 70 AD. The besieged community there battled an overwhelming Roman force for three years before choosing suicide rather than surrender. The Romans conquered only the bodies of this tribe; they did not conquer their spirits.

I do not remember where I read this last statement but it was many years ago, and I had never heard of Masada before. I was moved to write about the event in my notebook and have referred back to it over the years. I still don't know what I relate the story to, but I think if I could visit the location of what remains of Masada, I could interpret its true meaning from the ecclesiastical spirits still dwelling there.

ירים

I want to end my book at this time in an opened way because I want to continue to stir your mind. I just can't help myself. My astonishing teaching career is over, but I won't ever quit being an educator. My privilege to teach was and will always be a true blessing from God that I will be perpetually thankful for.

Thanks for reading and Good Luck!

Gracias por leer y Buen Suerte!

GLOSSARY

ADHD (ATTENTION DEFICIT HYPERACTIVE DISORDER): Chemicals in the brain cause this disability and it effects 5 to 10 % of children and can continue into adulthood. It interferes with a person's ability to pay attention and can result in inappropriate or unusual behavior. Medication can be used to help those with this disability.

ALTERNATIVE EDUCATION PROGRAM: A defined program that allows non-teacher, college graduates to go through a program to become some specific type of certified teacher. For example, they have programs for regular education, special education, or English as a Second Language. It was established in Texas as part of the 1984 Educational Reform Legislation. It provided for the training and certifying of high caliber teachers in districts where staffing needs could not be met through conventional teacher education programs.

ARD (ADMISSION, REVIEW, OR DISMISSAL): A term used in Texas for the meeting held one or more times a year for each Special Education student to discuss the student's progress and to establish Individual Education Goals. Meetings are also held to admit or dismiss students from special education. Those in attendance are the parents, the regular and special education teachers, the principle, therapists, and at times the nurse or whoever is or will be involved with the student.

Parents can also invite outside agencies or others to attend. All states have these meetings and procedures, but different terminology other than ARD can be used.

AUTISM: A developmental disorder that is defined by behaviors, including impaired social interaction, delayed and disordered language, and having isolated areas of interest. Much is not known about autism, but it's believed it is a disorder of the brain development beginning before birth. Causes are not fully defined, but genetics play a role, and environmental factors could also be involved. Autistic children may be unresponsive to people or focus intensely on one item. They may engage in repetitive movements or self-abusive behavior and don't know how to interact with other children. There is no known cure for autism, but therapies and behavior interventions may be designed to remedy specific symptoms and can bring about improvement. The majority of autistic children are male.

BLUE RIBBON SCHOOL: Founded in 1982, The National Blue Ribbon Schools Program recognizes public and private elementary, middle, and high schools where students perform at very high levels. A National Blue Ribbon School flag overhead has become a mark of excellence in education recognized by everyone from parents to policymakers in thousands of communities. Since the program's founding, the U.S. Department of Education has bestowed this coveted award on more than 7,000 of America's schools.

CHARTER SCHOOL: An alternative education system where a school receives public funding but is not contained by a government sanctioned curriculum. Public charter schools were authorized by the Texas Legislature in 1995 to provide more choice and option in public education. Texas has approximately 154,000 students on approximately 460 campuses across the state. Both charter and public school students take the state STAAR tests. Charter schools do not receive funds from local tax revenue, but they do receive an average of $1,500 less per student than independent school districts.

DISD (DALLAS INDEPENDENT SCHOOL DISTRICT): The 14th largest school district in the U.S. with over 158,000 students and approximately 20,000 employees including some 10,000 teachers.

DYSLEXIA: A reading disorder when the brain does not process letters correctly when reading. Most people with dyslexia have normal intelligence. Specific learning programs for dyslexia have been beneficial, especially when it's recognized early.

IEP (INDIVIDUAL EDUCATIONAL PLAN): Involves specific goal areas for each special education student. These are discussed and set at each annual ARD meeting. Sometimes there is more than one annual meeting and the IEP may be changed.

INCLUSION: When a special education teacher goes into the regular education class to work with one or more special education students. This process usually involves working with them in a group of regular education students in that class.

LEAST RESTRICTIVE ENVIRONMENT: Means the student who has the disability should have the opportunity to be educated with non-disabled peers to the greatest extent possible. They should have access to the general education curriculum or any program that non-disabled peers would be able to access.

LESSON PLAN: A teacher's detailed description of the course of instruction for one class. A daily lesson plan is developed to guide class instruction. In the past, details varied depending on the preference of the teacher and the need or curiosity of their student but now its content is mandated by the school system. (This required system is much more time consuming to make, and many teachers feel it is impractical for student learning compared to their own designed plans of the past)

LOW PERFORMING SCHOOL: A school that does not meet set specific standards in any one of several areas in the yearly state STAAR testing. For example, in Dallas, STAAR is categorized in the areas of economically disadvantaged, English as a second language, special education, or by race.

Occupational Therapist: A licensed person with a Master's Degree. They are usually a school district employee but can be a consultant. They treat students with disabilities through the therapeutic use of everyday activities. They help students develop, recover, and improve the skills needed for daily living and working.

Reading Coach: Coaches either work for the school district or as private consultants. They work with students on reading skills or with teachers to show and instruct them how to teach reading.

Resource Class: A special education class where the special education teacher brings the students into his or her class to work with them individually or in a group usually on reading or math. Usually the special education teacher plans the work but at times, the regular teacher may assign work.

School Administrators: Normally the term refers to those who do not teach or work directly with students. Please note, sometimes principals are referred to as school administrators, but for the purposes of this book, I felt it best not to include principals since they work with students every day.

School Board: In Dallas the board consists of five people who are elected for 4 year terms. They govern the whole Dallas school district by designating advisory committees holding regularly scheduled meetings. By the way, I was allowed to speak at one of these meetings but was limited to a three minute time limit.

School Sponsor: A company, church, or organization that sponsors a school and provides tutors and financial support, assists in school events, and provides for school needs. For example, sponsors might provide playground equipment or funds for a garden. They might even come to work with the students in the garden. Usually, only one school is taken by a sponsor, but I have seen a few individual sponsors involved with more than one school.

SCHOOL SUPERINTENDANT: The head of the whole school district and works with and is accountable to the school board. In most districts, the school board hires the superintendent.

SST (STUDENT SUPPORT TEAM): A team approach to discuss and propose solutions to students having difficulties in academics, behavior, or any other problems. The team consists of the regular and special education teachers, parents, principal, councilor, nurse, therapists if necessary, and two or three teachers or school staff who attend every SST meeting. In Dallas, it is termed SST. In other districts, it could be called by another name, but the principle of operation is similar.

STAAR TESTS (STATE OF TEXAS ASSESSMENT OF ACADEMIC READINGS): This is a program of tests given in the spring. The tests include annual assessments for grades 3 through 8 in reading and mathematics, assessments in writing at grades 4 through 7 and in science at grades 5 through 8. Specific high school tests are also required. Each state has its own set of tests in accordance with federal laws.

TEACCH (TREATMENT AND EDUCATION OF AUTISTIC AND RELATED COMMUNICATION HANDICAPPED CHILDREN): TEACCH classrooms utilize structural teaching with separate defined areas for each task, such as individual work, group activities, and play. It relies on visual learning and the student's use schedules made of pictures and words to order their day and to help them move smoothly between activities or to answer questions or make requests. Developed by the University of North Carolina in the 1960's for people with autism.

TEACHER OF THE YEAR: The person in each school elected annually by the school faculty for outstanding service.